FREE
from
PANIC

FREE FROM PANIC

A TEEN'S GUIDE TO COPING WITH PANIC ATTACKS AND PANIC SYMPTOMS

**Monika Parkinson,
Kerstin Thirlwall
and Lucy Willetts**

Illustrated by Richy K. Chandler

Jessica Kingsley Publishers
London and Philadelphia

First published in Great Britain in 2022 by Jessica Kingsley Publishers
An imprint of Hodder & Stoughton Ltd
An Hachette Company

1

A CIP catalogue record for this title is available from the British Library
and the Library of Congress

ISBN 978 1 78775 818 6
eISBN 978 1 78775 819 3

Jessica Kingsley Publishers' policy is to use papers that are natural,
renewable and recyclable products and made from wood grown
in sustainable forests. The logging and manufacturing processes
are expected to conform to the environmental regulations
of the country of origin.

Jessica Kingsley Publishers
Carmelite House
50 Victoria Embankment
London EC4Y 0DZ

www.jkp.com

The information contained in this book is not intended to replace
the services of trained medical professionals or to be a substitute
for medical advice. You are advised to consult a doctor on any
matters relating to your health, and in particular on any matters
that may require diagnosis or medical attention.

Contents

Chapter 1

Freedom Is Already Yours and We Will Show You Why

Hello and welcome

We are pleased you are reading this book in order to help you feel less overwhelmed by panic. Our hope is that you find this book easy to use and useful for both your current situation and future experiences. Whether you are a young person who is experiencing panic symptoms or a parent/carer or professional who wants to support a young person to feel better, it is our intention to give you a range of ideas and ways to gain freedom from panic.

We would like you to discover that freedom from panic is ALREADY YOURS and we will show you why and how. Many people often get caught up with doing a lot of different things to control and reduce their panic, which can keep the problem going and even make things much worse. Perhaps the most surprising thing that you will discover in this book is that the more you DO NOTHING ABOUT THE PANIC, the better you will feel. We hope to show you how to do nothing, drop the effort and let go of the need to control!

We refer to 'panic symptoms', 'anxiety' and 'anxiety symptoms or sensations' throughout this book. Although medical and diagnostic literature often defines these terms in particular ways, unless stated, we are not referring to these specific criteria in this book. Instead, we use language that includes panic, panic symptoms, anxiety and anxiety symptoms or sensations because we have found that these are commonly used by people to describe their experiences of panic. We would like you to use the word or words that best describe your feelings and experiences, without making things complicated.

What this book includes and how to use it

The content in this book is based on many years of our combined clinical practice with young people and families, as well as evidence-based approaches about helpful interventions. Having said that, we won't be giving you a ton of references or additional things to read, and we aim to provide our knowledge in the simplest and most usable way for you to apply quickly and effectively. You will notice that at the end of each chapter we have included a section called 'Questions to get you thinking'. Of course, it is up to you whether you complete these sections or not. In our experience, we've seen that if a person is able to set aside a few minutes to reflect on these questions, and even make some notes to refer to, this tends to increase the person's understanding of their symptoms and reactions and often leads to better results.

We also want to emphasize the importance of reading this book in the order it is presented, rather than dipping in and out of chapters. This is because we cover varying approaches, and there is a method in applying them in the order discussed. Following this structure helps to establish the building blocks for letting go of panic in an effective way. In particular, the ideas discussed in Chapters 4, 5 and 6 are crucial in establishing a foundation from which you can feel more confident and empowered to achieve freedom from panic. These chapters also present useful ways for coping with anxiety as well as other strong or negative feelings. Chapters 7 and 8 then go into more practical challenges with additional ideas to help you develop more helpful perspectives and responses. Our message is that you need to get to know your panic, your feelings and your body first before you can confidently let go of your panic symptoms in more specific situations.

What is panic?

Panic is no laughing matter. People often use the phrase 'don't panic' in a light-hearted way, but for those individuals who experience severe panic symptoms or panic disorder, this is much easier said than done. Panic symptoms, or a full panic attack, can often feel overwhelming and extremely frightening. Many people report feeling or thinking that they are about to collapse or die. Experiencing panic symptoms can make a person feel anxious a lot of the time, even when the panic has subsided, and it can lead to avoidance of certain situations, people or places and start to have a negative impact on many areas of life.

It is our hope that by the time you finish reading this book and understand some of the principles, you will be completely convinced, even whilst still perhaps experiencing some symptoms, that:

There is nothing wrong with you and this will pass.

When people talk about panic, they are usually referring to a number of physiological or bodily symptoms that can be experienced as a result of anxiety. For some people, the panic feelings are much more thought based, coming up as streams of anxious thoughts or distressing images. But for the most part, panic is usually experienced physically in our bodies. Panic symptoms can be very different for different individuals. On the next page we have put together a list of common symptoms that have been described by people of different ages.

For some people who experience panic on a regular basis, simply reading a list of symptoms like the ones here can actually start to bring on panic symptoms. If reading this list starts to make you feel a bit panicky, please remember this is natural and nothing to worry about. It is just an indication, like for all human beings, that your mind and your body are connected, and you are having a natural response to something that your mind finds scary at the moment. It actually demonstrates the amazing power of our thoughts and minds, and we can use that to our advantage in order to be more comfortable with these feelings (more on this in later chapters).

If you would prefer to skip over this list for now, please do so and return to it another time.

- Feeling light-headed
- Dizziness
- Blurred vision or altered vision
- Changes in hearing
- Tightness in throat or choking feeling
- Difficulty swallowing
- Dry mouth
- Racing or pounding heart
- Tightness or pain in the chest
- Difficulty breathing
- Tightness or stiffness in muscles
- Sweating
- Feeling sick in the stomach
- Stomach aches or butterflies
- Numbness or tingling in hands, feet, arms or legs
- Shakiness or trembling
- Feeling very hot or cold
- Weakness in legs or other muscles
- Feeling like you might faint
- Feeling like you are losing control or going crazy
- Feeling like you may die
- And other symptoms...

IMPORTANT MESSAGE

Panic symptoms are a natural response to something that your mind finds scary.

Some people might experience most of these symptoms all at once, and for others they may just experience a handful of these in different combinations. Or it can start with one symptom and then escalate into further symptoms rising up over time. Panic symptoms can last for a few moments, for several minutes or sometimes for longer periods of time. They can pop up at any time, out of the blue, in the day or at night. They can also be experienced in more predictable situations where they have happened before, such as in crowds, in class, on public transport or in small spaces.

What is the difference between panic and panic disorder?

When professionals talk about panic disorder, they are referring to a set of symptoms according to particular criteria that have been established by scientists and clinicians. This way of describing panic symptoms helps professionals to understand how much the panic is disrupting a person's life and whether it fits our understanding of the disorder. If you are interested in these criteria, we have included the details of a Royal College of Psychiatrists website at the end of this book.

For the purpose of using this book, it does not matter whether you meet these criteria for panic disorder or not. If you are experiencing a few or many panic symptoms on a regular basis and you want to find ways to feel calmer, then the chapters in this book will likely be helpful to you.

A note about other difficulties

Panic symptoms can be experienced on their own or can sit alongside a range of other different emotional and physical difficulties. For example, some people with other anxieties, such as phobias or fears about social situations, report sometimes having intense panic symptoms. Others with low mood or those people who have experienced a traumatic event may experience regular symptoms of panic. There are also some physical conditions that can trigger or give rise to panic-like symptoms, such as sensory sensitivities, an over-active thyroid or cardiovascular problems.

Our advice to anyone reading this book is to chat to your usual healthcare provider, such as your general practitioner (GP), about your panic symptoms to rule out any specific physical causes first.

In addition, if your panic symptoms are related to a very frightening or a traumatic event, or if they are connected to other anxiety problems that are more troubling to you (such as fears in social situations), we suggest that you seek support for these difficulties first before using this book for the panic symptoms. And of course, if your panic is so severe that it is stopping you from being able to take part fully in everyday life, then we strongly urge you, in addition to using this book, to get the right support in place from a psychologist or mental health professional. We have given some suggestions of where to find further help at the back of this book.

Round up

We hope that you are interested and even inspired to learn more about your feelings and that we have given you hope that freedom from your panic is within your reach.

Questions to get you thinking

In this section we invite you to reflect on your current situation and to make some notes about some of your experiences. Have a think about what symptoms you tend to experience when you feel panicky. Use the list earlier to help you think about your own feelings.

1. *What is my panic like?*

2. *What symptoms do I experience when I feel panicky?*

....

....

....

3. *How long has this been going on for?*

4. *What situations seem to bring these symptoms on? Or do they come out of the blue when I'm not even expecting them?*

5. *How often do I experience panic?*

6. *How long do the symptoms tend to last?*

7. *How severe are the symptoms? (0 = completely fine, 10 = the most anxious you have felt)*

8. *Am I thinking anything when feeling panicky? If yes, what am I thinking might happen?*

9. *How do I cope? In what ways do I try to control my panic or the situations where it arises?*

10. *What seems to help me?*

If you are ready and willing to discover some new ideas about your panic, then we invite you to carry on reading this book and working your way through the chapters in order. We are confident that as you work through, you will begin to uncover your freedom from your panic.

Chapter 2
So Basically
You're Just Normal

As we have already discussed, your *mind and body are connected*, and panic symptoms are a *natural response to something that your mind finds scary*. This idea is incredibly important because it forms the basis of why we invite you to stop doing all the things you currently do and why we instead will show you ways of letting go. When you are experiencing panic symptoms, however, we know it can be incredibly difficult to believe that they will pass and that you don't need to do anything.

For this reason, we are dedicating a whole chapter to sharing with you why panic symptoms (although experienced in varying levels of intensity and frequency) are, in fact, normal and something we can all experience.

Although panic symptoms are impossible to ignore, once you know the truth about why they show up, you may then find that they are less frightening and don't happen quite so often.

To better convince you that what you are going through is normal, we are going to share with you some important information about how the human brain developed, and in particular some important information about why you might experience more anxiety and panic symptoms in your teenage years. This is a topic that could easily fill an entire book, but we are going to focus on the things that we feel are most relevant to helping you free yourself from panic.

How the human brain developed and why this makes things hard

Many of us assume that positive mental health should come naturally. If someone experiences high levels of anxiety or another kind of mental health challenge, you may think that perhaps they didn't take care of themselves the right way, or maybe there is something 'wrong' with them that needs to be fixed or solved in order for them to feel better. If so, it may surprise you to learn that a large amount of psychological distress happens because of the way the human brain evolved.

Once you know more about how the human brain developed, you realize that panic symptoms, along with uncomfortable emotions and upsetting thoughts, are an unavoidable part of being human.

The three systems

To better understand this, we would like you to start thinking of your brain as having three separate systems: one that we share with all other species (the primitive part of our brain), another that we share with many other members of the animal kingdom (such as mammals) and the third system, which forms our higher intelligence (exclusive to us humans).

Each of these systems of our brain are built on the foundations of the others, and although they are very different, they share a common purpose: they want to keep us alive.

All of our human experiences (including panic) are the result of these different parts of the brain trying to get along and serve us as best they can. But, as you will see, through no fault of our own, our brains can make things harder than they need to be.

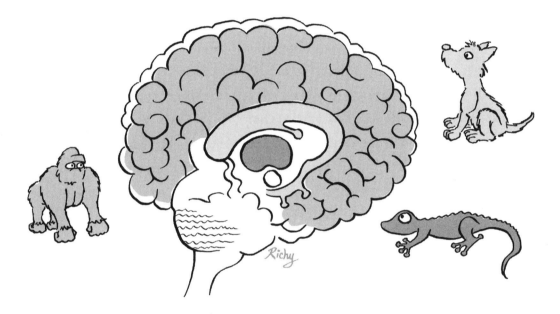

The reptilian brain (primitive system)
– all it wants is to keep you alive

Let's start by introducing the oldest part of our brain and what is commonly referred to as 'the reptilian brain'. As you may have guessed from its name, it is the part of our brain that we have in common with reptiles, but also with all other living creatures. The reptilian brain is thought to have first appeared in fish around 500 million years ago. This part of the brain controls all the vital bodily functions required to keep us alive, depending on what is going on around us (e.g., by regulating our heart rate, breathing and body temperature). It is an automatic and reliable system, but it is also very rigid and stubborn.

Our rigid reptile brain is only concerned with keeping us alive (e.g. by regulating our temperature, breathing, digestive system and heart rate depending on what is needed in the moment).

The good news is that we don't need to 'think' about telling our heart to beat quicker when we are in dangerous situations. Our reptilian brain knows exactly what our body needs to do when we are in danger. These temporary changes to our bodily functions when threat is detected are known as our *'fight or flight' responses*.

Below is an overview of our most common 'fight or flight' responses and the reasons behind them. As you look over these, there is a high chance that you will notice the similarities between these responses and your panic symptoms. In fact, if you go back to Chapter 1, you will see that they are more or less identical to what many people experience as panic!

We could just leave things here – after all, our 'fight or flight' response already explains a lot about why we may experience panic symptoms. But although you might agree that your 'fight or flight' response makes sense when you are in danger, you may be wondering how this can explain your panic symptoms when there isn't any physical danger. Typically, it is during these times that people think there must be something wrong and want to control or fix their panic in some way.

Even when there is no danger, it is still normal for your body to activate 'fight or flight' responses.

The reason for this becomes clearer when you learn about the other regions of the brain and the role they play. So please read on.

Racing thoughts – rapid thinking helps us to evaluate and problem-solve how to escape danger quicker. This makes it very difficult to concentrate or focus on anything apart from danger or escape options

Changes to vision – sharper vision so you can pay more attention to danger

Nausea and butterflies in stomach – blood diverted away from digestive system

Needing the toilet – muscles in bladder relax to eliminate excess weight

Sweaty palms or under arms – sweating to keep body cool whilst it is being overworked

Dizzy/light-headed – excess levels of oxygen not used up if not running away or fighting

Dry mouth – saliva production stops as digestive system is shut down to divert energy to muscles

Breathing quicker and shallower – taking in more oxygen to power the muscles

Heart beats faster – more blood is circulated to muscles to help you fight or run away

Hands get cold – blood vessels in skin contract to force blood towards muscles

Tense muscles and shaking – muscles ready to run away or fight. May also shake or tremble as a way of getting ready for action

Richy

The mammalian brain (limbic system) – it wants us to form relationships

The next part of the brain to evolve was the mammalian brain, which we have in common with all mammals. This system is responsible for our social behaviours and emotional experiences. It records memories, guides us towards making friends and tries to direct us towards making safe and loving relationships.

When you were born, like all mammals, you relied on a caregiver to provide your basic needs (milk, comfort and exploration). Although we become increasingly independent, even as we get older, our food, living arrangements and daily tasks continue to be heavily influenced by the people around us. We continue to rely on the acceptance and closeness of others to keep us alive. If you have ever felt that warm and fuzzy feeling when someone seems to 'get' you or found yourself attracted to and wanting to be close to another person, then that's your limbic system supporting one of our deepest biological needs: to love and be loved by others.

Unfortunately, when we think other people don't like us or we have had a negative social interaction, the downside is that we can experience a high level of distress. This can also happen if we simply don't have enough experiences of positive social activities. Specifically, we get a rush of uncomfortable emotions. These are intended to protect us and motivate us into doing something to stay safe, but they can be incredibly unpleasant and aren't always accurate.

The mammalian brain gives us our strong desire for relationships and our need to belong to a group. It is responsible for creating emotions to try to keep us connected to groups and remain safe.

Here are some common unpleasant emotions people often feel alongside episodes of panic, and what their intended purpose is.

Emotion	Intended action	Intended purpose
Fear	Get away/avoid	Safety
Anger	Attack	Safety
Sadness	Slow down	Give your body rest from 'fight or flight' state and try something different
Shame/embarrassment	Hide/cover up	Gain social approval
Guilt	Make amends	Gain social approval

Primate and human system (neocortex) – it thinks about everything!

The last system to evolve was the neocortex, which led to the primate brain, and then finally to the brain us humans know today. There is still a lot we are learning about the neocortex, but one of the things we know for certain is that our neocortex has given us our unique intelligence and advantage over other species. For example, our neocortex allows us to problem-solve, make comparisons, learn from our mistakes and plan ahead. In contrast to our reptilian system, this advanced structure is adaptable and flexible, and some say it has no limits at all.

The human brain allows us to think about our experiences (e.g. to monitor our actions, make judgments, imagine what can happen, make comparisons and go over what has happened in the past). It allows us to defeat danger through intellect rather than relying on physical strength alone. It has no limits in terms of its creativity and imagination.

The trouble with connection

You might think that having a superior, more advanced brain would lead to a life of endless security and gratitude, but there are very few people who can say this has been their reality.

Although all three systems try the best they can to work together as a team, they can set each other off in very unhelpful ways. We spend a lot of our time living our life through our minds: thinking about things and trying to solve everything or figure everything out. Often we are not aware of what our brain is doing and, as you will discover in the next chapter, it is very easy to become trapped in panic for this very reason.

Have a read of the story below and see if you can recognize the three separate systems at play. See if you can spot the ways in which Jack's survival instincts are influencing his physical, emotional and behavioural responses. In particular, try to see how his mammalian brain (need for social connection) and human brain (ability to think and reflect about events) activate his reptilian brain's 'fight or flight' responses (or panic symptoms).

Feel free to use the lines provided underneath to write down any notes as you go along.

Jack is walking along the street with a group of friends. As he turns a corner, a big, aggressive dog suddenly starts barking and lunging at him. He jumps and lets out a momentary squeal. Immediately after, Jack feels stupid. He notices that the dog is muzzled and on a short leash, and he feels his face going red. He mutters to himself, 'A dog like that shouldn't be allowed out in public.' His friend Paul asks if he is all right. His other two friends, Steven and Kai, laugh and start teasing him. Jack ignores them, and the four boys start talking about something else.

Later that evening, Jack's mum asks him how his day was. Jack suddenly remembers the incident and starts complaining to his mum about how he was almost attacked by a dog. As he tells her the story, his voice becomes louder, his temperature rises and he starts to feel sweaty. He shares his frustration over the dog owner and says there should be a law about when to walk dogs. His mum tells him that will never happen and that it's not worth getting upset over.

Jack finishes his day in bed, scrolling through his social media and checking what he has planned tomorrow. He looks at his phone and sees a group message about football club tomorrow. Jack remembers that his mum isn't able to drive him this week. He starts thinking about his route and the best way to get there. He wonders whether he will need to walk the same street as he did today. Jack puts his phone down and tries to fall asleep. As he lies in bed, he imagines what he would do if he saw the same dog and owner again. He thinks to himself, 'What if the owner heard me and talks back to me?' and 'What if everyone starts to laugh at me again?' Then he becomes annoyed with himself: 'I was so stupid. Why did I have to scream?' Jack starts to feel restless and notices butterflies in his stomach. He finds it impossible to shake off the feeling that his friends think he is a loser. Who else might they tell? How many times has he done something stupid? As he lies in his bed, wide awake, Jack looks at the time and notices that he has been awake for most of the night. He becomes upset about how tired he is going to be in the morning. 'I'll probably play really rubbish tomorrow, then everyone will really hate me.' He reaches for his phone and sends Paul a message to tell him that he won't make football practice tomorrow.

....

....

....

Knowing about the different parts of our brain and having read the story above, we hope you can better understand what we told you in Chapter 1: that panic symptoms are a natural response to something that your mind finds scary. Just like in the story above, all of us have a brain that activates 'fight or flight' responses, even when the situation turns out to be safe. Although Jack was never in any real danger, his body got him ready for action. This happened before he was able to assess the situation, but once the process had begun, the other parts of his brain quickly played their role in trying to keep him safe too. He formed a judgment about what occurred ('Dogs like that shouldn't be allowed in public!' 'My friends think I'm stupid.') and experienced a sudden change in his emotions (fear, embarrassment and anger). Even once he was safely back at home, simply thinking about his experience was enough to alter his body temperature and bring up strong emotions. When he started to think about the next day, Jack automatically started thinking about the possibility of the same thing happening again and started evaluating all the things that could go wrong. He went into 'problem-solving mode' and was no longer able to rest. His mind and body continued to prepare themselves for the possibility of danger, and eventually the urge to escape led to him cancelling his plans.

The MORE Jack did in response to his symptoms, the WORSE his anxiety got.

We will talk more about how our responses to things trigger panic and keep it going in the next chapter, but hopefully understanding more about how your brain works helps you to see why panic symptoms can come up so easily, and that, although they are never pleasant, they aren't your fault, and if they do come up, there is a reason.

Our 'fight or flight' responses occur during times of danger AND whenever we think about potential danger. Our evaluations, self-criticism and judgments all keep the feeling of fear going and can give rise to these unpleasant physical responses, even when there is no obvious external threat.

The above is particularly true when we are in periods of stress and can feel even more intense during our teenage years. The reason for this, as you will discover in the final section of this chapter, is that your brain is undergoing a particularly important transformation during this time. If you speak to some adults in your life and ask them about their own teenage years, you will probably hear some wonderful stories as they recall their younger years. No doubt, they will also remember the intense feelings and physical changes that made everything seem more difficult too.

The turbulence of teenage years – sometimes you really are going backwards

One of the reasons everything can become so much harder during your adolescent years is that your brain is going through a massive growth spurt – and it does this back to front, just like it did when you were an infant. The first parts to grow are the regions connected to the reptilian and mammalian systems. As such, the part of your brain involved in automatic, impulsive and emotional reactions becomes dominant and used the most. As you now know, it will be great at keeping you alive but cannot be relied upon to help you make sensible, balanced decisions. In order to think logically and consider all the options and consequences of your behaviour, you need to make more use of the neocortex. This region does not begin its growth spurt until later, however, and continues to lag behind until the human brain reaches full maturity at around 25 years of age.

We are not at all suggesting that you lack intelligence during your teenage years. In fact, a huge amount of growth has already happened in all areas of our brain by the time we are seven years of age. Instead, until the neocortex catches up, you may find that your thinking and problem-solving becomes heavily influenced by your survival instincts and emotions. If so, that's okay and a normal part of growing up.

During the adolescent years, you may not read situations accurately or respond to things in the most helpful way. You may frequently find that things don't quite turn out as you thought they would, and you may become less trusting that things will be okay.

During this time, decisions are often based on whether something feels good or bad, rather than on the consequences of an action that you have thought through. You may have heard others talk about teenagers as being impulsive or noticed yourself that you or your friends are more likely than adults to do things that feel good in the moment that you later regret or that get you into trouble. Additionally, you may avoid doing things that would actually be helpful in the long run.

Again, this isn't your fault, but as you continue to read this book, we will share with you some proven ways in which you can reduce some of these responses, as well as your panic symptoms, by increasing your ability to stop, reflect and develop more balanced thinking – even as your brain goes through this tricky transformation. Not only will working on this now help you through your adolescent years but also your adult self will thank you for taking the time to learn these skills sooner rather than later.

Round up

We hope that this chapter has convinced you that panic symptoms can be understood as a normal part of being human and that the adolescent years are a time when you may find yourself particularly vulnerable to higher levels of anxiety and physical discomfort.

Questions to get you thinking

1. *What are your most common 'fight or flight' responses? How would these physical responses help you if you were in danger?*

2. *Our fear reactions are built upon a 'better to be safe than sorry' system. How regularly do you go back to check the facts that your reptilian brain may have missed?*

3. *What are some of the drawbacks of having an advanced brain?*

4. *Are there times when you find yourself overthinking or making something seem bigger than what it really is?*

5. *When do you find yourself becoming emotional? Are there times when acting on feelings has ended up being unhelpful?*

Chapter 3

But Why Do You Get Trapped by Your Panic?

So panic symptoms are actually a normal part of how your brain works. We also know that, in adolescence, you are more likely to experience anxiety and feelings of physical discomfort and to make decisions and act on these feelings rather than stopping to think things through. But you may be asking yourself, Why do I get these feelings so often, and why are they so bad? Why don't other people I know get them too? Why do they feel so scary if they are actually normal? Why don't they just go away when the danger has passed, and why do they happen at all if there is no danger? These are really important and valid questions to ask. The simple answer is: you feel uncomfortable about feeling uncomfortable, and you try to fight and battle against this by controlling and/or running away. This is completely understandable. We will spend this chapter explaining this reaction in more detail and later show you that dropping this battle will help you feel better.

We are going to talk more about anxiety, what it looks like and how it leads us to think and behave. Our thinking and our behaviour are crucial and can actually keep the panic symptoms going. This is not your fault; this is how our brain works when we feel anxious. But you can make changes in the way you think and react.

Why do some people struggle with panic symptoms and some don't?

Well, to start with, some people are simply more prone to having anxiety than others. We all experience anxiety – we all have the 'fight or flight' response, and we know from the last chapter that this is an important part of how our brain works. It keeps us safe. However, for some, this is triggered when there isn't actually any danger, as Jack found out in the last chapter.

Some young people will experience panic symptoms much more often than other people.

The other thing to bear in mind is that panic symptoms are not always that obvious on the outside. You may think they are, because when you feel them they are so unpleasant, but on the outside they can actually be pretty subtle. You wouldn't necessarily know that someone's heart is beating fast or that their stomach is churning. So, there may actually be a whole load of people in your school who do often have panic symptoms but it's simply not apparent to anyone around them.

What about anxiety in general? Where does it come from?

But why are some people more prone to anxiety? Genes play a part; we inherit all sorts of things from our parents, and a tendency to get anxious may be one of them. Environment is another factor; we learn from people around us. If someone close to us sees danger and threat (where there might not be any), we also may begin to see threat too. Here is an example: your mum sees a large spider, she screams and she leaves the room. This happens repeatedly. As a young child, this may lead you to think, 'Hey, spiders must be dangerous in some way. I had better avoid them too!' Life events and difficult experiences may also play a part. For example, you are involved in a car crash, or someone close to you dies. This may lead you to seeing the world a bit differently. You realize that people do die, even people close to you, and that changes how you behave somewhat. People may treat you differently because of this; teachers may think you need special treatment, they may make allowances for you or they perhaps don't push you as much to do well. In essence, they protect you more. All these things contribute to the chances of any of us experiencing anxiety.

There are lots of things that influence how prone we are to anxiety.

What does anxiety look like, and how does it work?

So you can see that some of us are simply more prone to developing anxiety than others; our brains will see danger or threat more quickly and more readily than others and react to this. Our 'fight or flight' system is then activated, and we experience a range of unpleasant physical feelings, which you probably know as panic symptoms. Remember, though, from the last chapter, that these sensations are actually normal and can be helpful.

They only become a problem if they are interpreted as dangerous or harmful, or if we think we can't cope with them.

Anxiety is not just physical feelings, however. Anxiety is made up of thoughts and behaviours too. We experience anxious thoughts or worries when we are anxious, and we behave in a certain way in reaction to our anxious thoughts and feelings. Our anxious thoughts usually tell us something bad is going to happen (e.g. I might get a bad mark in this exam; I will do something embarrassing) or they might tell us that we won't be able to cope with whatever happens (e.g. if I am sick, I won't know what to do; if I get anxious, I won't be able to cope). When we feel anxious, our brain is great at persuading us that our anxious thoughts are most definitely true or will come true, even though the chances of this happening are usually very small. We call this an 'attentional bias'. Our brain gets us to focus on all the information that backs up our worry or anxious thought, and in doing so, it means we don't spot any information to the contrary. Don't forget, your brain is built on trying to secure your survival, so it often operates on a 'better to be safe than sorry' principle and doesn't want to miss any potential danger.

Anxious thoughts about panic symptoms...

As we talked about in Chapter 1, panic symptoms almost always come with anxious thoughts too. Given that you are reading this book, I am sure we don't need to tell you how unpleasant these physical symptoms are, and that therefore, understandably, we become fearful of them in their own right.

Here are some anxious thoughts young people have about their panic symptoms:

- They are a sign that I am having a heart attack.

- I can't breathe; I might die.

- I might faint.

- They mean I am seriously ill.

- I will lose control (and might do something awful or embarrassing).

- They won't stop and will last forever.

- They mean I'm going mad.

- People will think I'm crazy.

Write a list of any other anxious thoughts/interpretations that you notice yourself having about your panic symptoms:

1. ....

2. ....

3. ....

4. ....

These thoughts make the problem bigger. You see these physical sensations as dangerous, not just unpleasant – this is our reptilian brain in action again. That inevitably leads to more physical symptoms, which in turn leads to more anxious thoughts, and so the panic cycle keeps going.

Anxious thoughts or interpretations about the panic symptoms make them worse and keep them going.

Anxious behaviour – what we do when we panic

Panic symptoms also lead to you behaving in a certain way. Our anxious behaviour usually involves us trying to avoid the thing that makes us anxious or brings on the panic symptoms (e.g. I can't do the test; I am not going to the party). This is the 'flight' part of our biological reaction that we talked about in Chapter 2.

Our instinct is to get away or keep away from the thing that makes us feel anxious. You may point out, though, that your panic symptoms sometimes seem to come out of the blue. And you are right; they often do. If that is the case, or if we can't avoid the situation that triggered our panic symptoms, we do other things to try to keep ourselves safe, for example trying to control our breathing or find ways of getting rid of the panic symptoms. These are also anxious behaviours, and they play a big part in keeping our panic symptoms going. They make us believe we were only safe because we did something to reduce our unpleasant feelings. We call these 'panic traps' because this is our panic trapping us into doing things that we don't actually need to do.

Panic traps are our panic trapping us into doing things that we don't actually need to do and that keep our panic symptoms going.

Another form of avoidance is trying to avoid a whole range of unpleasant emotions. We might try to push these away or distract ourselves so that we forget about them. This can work, but it can also just mean these emotions build up and might result in some panic symptoms that appear to come out of the blue but are actually triggered by feelings we want to avoid.

So, in essence, anxious thoughts, behaviours and physical sensations work together to trigger panic symptoms and keep them going. These panic cycles, where a trigger leads to perceived danger, physical sensations, anxious thoughts and panic traps, can happen in a variety of situations. Let's follow along with Maria, a young person who experiences these cycles at school.

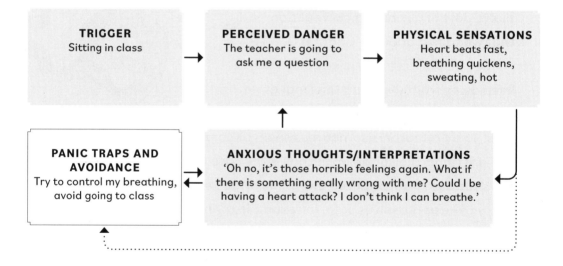

My panic symptoms cycle

Have a go at completing your own panic cycle. If you don't know what your triggers are, leave that blank for now. As you reflect about your panic, you may discover particular subtle triggers in time.

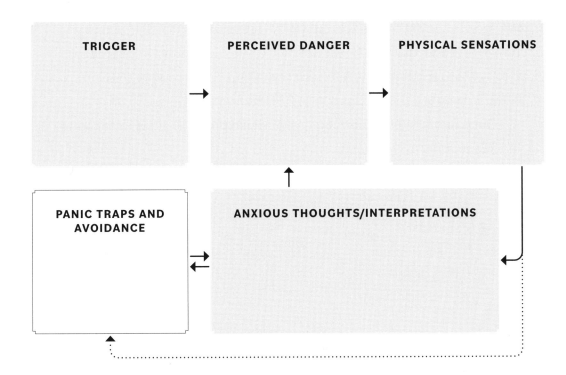

Why do panic symptoms sometimes happen out of the blue?

Although panic symptoms are sometimes triggered by a specific situation – we will come to this later – they often occur out of the blue. This is a particular puzzle to many young people. Why do I get these feelings when I am not in a scary situation? Why do I get these feelings when I am not worrying or thinking about anything that makes me feel anxious?

One reason for this is that your brain starts to be 'on the lookout' for unpleasant or worrying physical sensations. We call this 'hypervigilance'. If we go back to the reptilian brain and the 'fight or flight' response, we know that there are times when we are on the lookout for danger, and that this is actually helpful. Think of cavemen hunting: they would have been on the lookout for dangerous animals so that they could react in time to either kill them or run away.

We start to do the same with physical sensations. Any sign of one, however small, and our brain notices it. We also know that some people tend to notice these physical feelings more readily than others. They are more tuned in to how their body feels.

Once our brain has noticed one of these physical signs, it tends to lead to a panic cycle.

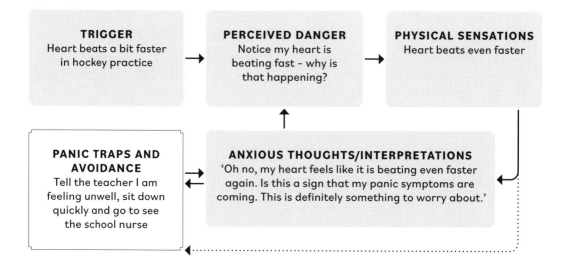

In this example, the trigger is a normal increase in heart beat due to physical activity. But Maria's brain sees it as dangerous and the panic cycle starts. There are lots of situations that lead to us experiencing physical sensations of some sort or another, including feeling physically unwell, any sort of physical exercise, feeling a bit hot, having low blood sugar... Your brain might spot any of these physical symptoms and see them as a sign of danger.

But I don't know what my triggers are

Sometimes we may not even be aware of what our triggers are. They might be so subtle or so quick that our reptilian brain perhaps registers a trigger before we have even had a chance to know it's happening.

Our brain sometimes interprets normal physical sensations as dangerous.

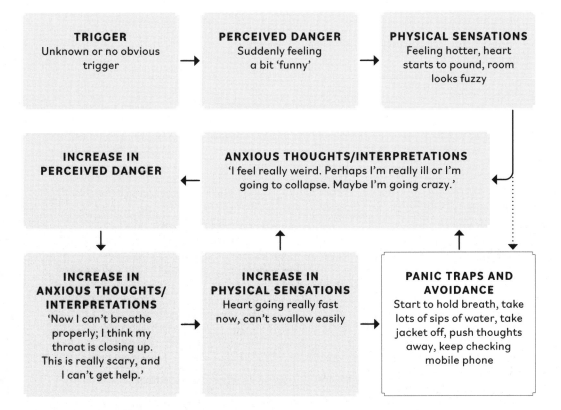

We mentioned another reason for out of the blue panic above - the idea that we sometimes try to suppress or avoid difficult emotions and push them away. If we do this a lot, it may mean those emotions can come out in a physical way, hence we notice more panic symptoms. This same principle appears when we are exposed to more and more stress. Things build up and up, and eventually even a very small thing can lead to a 'fight or flight' response - our panic symptoms. So even though it feels like our panic came out of the blue, it didn't.

Specific situations also trigger panic symptoms

Sometimes panic symptoms are triggered by a particular situation. This could be any situation but is usually a situation where you feel or have previously felt anxious for some reason – sitting a test, doing a presentation, being in a place that is hard to get out of (a lesson, assembly, the cinema)... the list goes on.

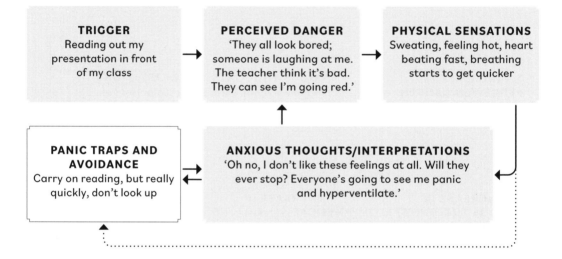

TRIGGER
Reading out my presentation in front of my class

PERCEIVED DANGER
'They all look bored; someone is laughing at me. The teacher think it's bad. They can see I'm going red.'

PHYSICAL SENSATIONS
Sweating, feeling hot, heart beating fast, breathing starts to get quicker

PANIC TRAPS AND AVOIDANCE
Carry on reading, but really quickly, don't look up

ANXIOUS THOUGHTS/INTERPRETATIONS
'Oh no, I don't like these feelings at all. Will they ever stop? Everyone's going to see me panic and hyperventilate.'

Reading out in front of the class triggers Maria's anxiety. Her brain perceives this situation as threatening or dangerous, as she is worried about being judged negatively by her peers and teacher. She then notices some physical sensations. This is her reptilian brain in action. Maria would really like to get up and leave, as she continues to worry about the class looking bored or someone laughing, but now she would also like to escape these unpleasant feelings – her mammalian brain at work. Maria doesn't feel she can leave, though (she might get into trouble from the teacher or someone might ask why she is going), so she keeps presenting and tries to get it over with quickly. So Maria's neocortex is now in action, trying to problem-solve for her. It is only when Maria eventually finishes her presentation that her anxiety reduces – the physical sensations go away, and her anxious thoughts start to disappear.

You can probably think of situations that trigger your panic symptoms. Write down as many as you can think of below. We will come back to these in Chapter 8 when we start to build a plan to free you from your panic. Don't worry if you don't know what your triggers are, though. Sometimes it takes a while to realize exactly what may be triggering panic.

1. ....

2. ....

3. ....

4. ....

5. ....

6. ....

7. ....

8. ....

Once we have felt anxious in a situation, understandably we often worry we will feel anxious in that situation again. We also begin to worry that the same panic symptoms will show up again.

Maria is now worried about her next presentation. *What if I get anxious again? What if I get all those horrible physical feelings?* Maria decides that she is going to try to get out of the next presentation because she can't face it. She also starts to feel anxious about going back into the same class, just in case she feels like that again.

Anxious thoughts/interpretations, anxious behaviour AND THE PANIC SYMPTOMS now keep her anxiety going.

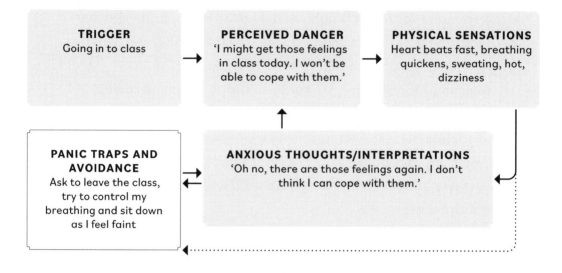

This time it is not the presentation that Maria perceives as dangerous but the class itself, as she is now worried about getting the physical sensations if she goes to her class again. When Maria leaves the class, she feels better. So, leaving the class seems like a good thing to do, and she does it every time she gets the panic symptoms. So, avoidance is now keeping Maria's panic going.

Maria also tries to control her breathing and sits down: her panic traps. Lots of people use them (and they are in fact sometimes actively encouraged). But Maria now thinks that her panic symptoms only stopped because she controlled them with breathing, and she only managed not to faint by sitting down. So her panic has effectively trapped her into doing these things again (and again). She begins to use her panic traps every time she gets panic symptoms.

Write down a list of your panic traps (things you do to control your panic symptoms or that help you feel safe or less anxious). We will come back to these in Chapter 8.

1. ....

2. ....

3. ....

4. ....

5. ....

6. ....

Panic traps and avoidance play a big part in maintaining panic.

Round up

Some people are more likely to struggle with panic symptoms than others. Panic symptoms can come out of the blue (although there may be a subtle trigger) or be triggered by particular situations. Avoiding situations that trigger panic symptoms and using panic traps both keep the cycle going. In the next five chapters, read about how you can begin to stop this panic cycle and move towards freedom from panic.

Questions to get you thinking

1. *Have you had any experiences or influences that might have made you more prone to anxiety?*

2. *Do your panic symptoms come mainly out of the blue or are they triggered by particular situations, or both?*

3. *What do you notice about those anxious thoughts/interpretations that often come with the physical feelings?*

4. *What do you do when you panic? Do you try to avoid stuff?*

5. *Do you try to control your panic sensations? What are your traps?*

6. *Are there things you do that are helpful, or perhaps things that keep your panic cycle going?*

Chapter 4
Accepting and Embracing Your Panic

Hopefully the first few chapters have shown you that fundamentally there is nothing wrong with you when you get panicky and anxious; it is a natural human response. In addition, you discovered that certain ways of thinking about different symptoms and situations, or responding in controlling ways in response to your symptoms, may actually be making those symptoms worse.

Now, you might be thinking that the title of this chapter is rather odd. Why would we suggest you accept or even embrace your panic? Isn't the whole idea to get rid of it? Well, yes, that's perhaps the ultimate goal, but as you have just read in Chapter 3, panic is one of those interesting things where the more you *try* to get rid of it, the more it can get bigger and stick around. Let us explain this a little bit more.

Letting go of the need to control

Panic symptoms, a bit like anxious or difficult thoughts, seem to get worse for people when they try hard to control them or to get rid of them. Let's start with thoughts. Try this little activity:

For ten seconds do whatever you can not to think about your bedroom. Go on, do whatever it takes to NOT think about how your bedroom looks and what is in there.
   What did you experience?

Many people report that when they try not to think about something, it pops into their mind straight away and then usually it just won't go away for a while.

   This is a natural phenomenon. When we try not to think about something, we end up thinking about it more. The same goes for some anxiety and panic symptoms. When you try to not feel panicky, this can end up making you feel more panicky. The reason for this is that when we try to control something like feelings and bodily sensations, it brings more of our *attention* to them, and this usually makes us more likely to feel those things with greater intensity. Sometimes, when we try to control particular symptoms or sensations, such as our breathing or how our muscles feel, we may end up creating more tension in those body areas, and this can lead to more unpleasant symptoms.

   This can also lead us to have more thoughts about the sensations and feelings, which again can fuel the symptoms. You may recall the cycle in Chapter 3. Once we notice our panic symptoms, this can give rise to more anxious thoughts and anxious behaviours, and then more panic symptoms, and around we go in a panic cycle.

Our responses to our feelings really matter

The idea of *accepting* or even *embracing* difficult feelings and sensations is not new. Thousands of years ago, many old scriptures described practices such as meditation, being in the present moment, acceptance, mindfulness, being with the self and with what is and so on. The truth is that humans are very complex creatures with amazing minds and imaginations. We are capable of so many wonderful things, and one of the most amazing things is that we can think about our thinking. Think about it! We can actually think about our own thoughts and feelings. That's pretty amazing. You can see, though, that when we are not feeling so good, this ability can sometimes let us down and make us feel worse.

Here are some examples of when it might not be helpful:

1. You feel a bit sad on a particular day, perhaps because your friends haven't been in touch and you feel a little lonely. You start to think about why you are feeling sad and so tired. Then you tell yourself to snap out of it. You start to get annoyed with yourself for feeling low, yet again. You tell yourself that you really should be more energetic, and you shouldn't just sit around. You think about all the other times you have felt low recently. You start to think that you are not like other people; others seem to be much happier. You tell yourself not to be so silly, and you start to wonder what is wrong with you. You tell yourself just to stop feeling so low, and you try to push the feelings away. Pretty quickly, you start to feel worse.

2. You feel yourself start to get a bit panicky. You know this is what is happening because it has happened before, and you now understand that these are your panic symptoms. You think, 'Oh no, here we go again.' You tell yourself to stop feeling this way or to get out of the place you're in. You think it's going to get worse, and it will never go away. You start to have thoughts that this is ruining your day; it's probably

ruining your life. You wish you were different. You try to control the feelings in various ways. You notice yourself getting more tense, and you wish it would all just disappear. You start to get really worried that there actually is something wrong with you. Pretty soon the panic symptoms start to get worse, and you feel bad about yourself.

Some of you may be able to relate to the two examples above. There are many other examples of times when we feel bad in some way, and by trying to push our feelings away, we end up making ourselves feel worse. This is because feelings that are pushed away or suppressed tend not to go away, and sometimes they come back in other ways like irritability, being really snappy or feeling low. Pushing feelings away can be like throwing another layer of bad feelings on top.

A common metaphor that is used to explain this is the quicksand metaphor. When someone finds themselves sinking in quicksand, the more they struggle and push against it, the faster they sink. This is a natural response and yet, counter to our instincts, a completely different approach is needed to help the person not to sink deeper. This might include slowing down, stopping the struggle, lying back and staying still. We can apply this to the way we can respond to our difficult feelings as well, as demonstrated further below.

Other ways that people try to push feelings away include using distraction activities too much, especially when the distraction involves unhelpful activities such as excessive gaming, social media use, television watching, eating junk food or taking substances such as alcohol or drugs. Sometimes even positive activities, such as sports or socializing, can be unhelpful if they are done to extreme levels and if the purpose is to avoid feelings and avoid thinking about feelings. Pleasurable and engaging activities are incredibly important for good mental health and for a balanced life, but they are bad news if the only reason you're doing them is to push your feelings away time after time. It is important to acknowledge feelings first, to accept that this is what you are feeling in the particular moment and then to see if you can restore some balance (Chapter 6) or engage in something that you know will calm or refresh you.

Try this instead

Now we'd like you to consider a completely different approach to the ones above. Rather than *rejecting*, *avoiding* and *pushing* feelings and sensations away, we suggest that you start to *notice*, *accept* and even *embrace* them. That way, you are sure not to be adding this extra layer of bad feelings and thoughts, and there's less chance of them building up and sneaking up on you. Also, with practice, you may find that you will be more able to *tolerate* your difficult feelings and they will pass more quickly.

1.   Notice your feelings.

2.   Accept them and stay with what is.

3.   Embrace what is happening rather than trying to avoid it or push it away.

4.   Be nice to yourself about it (more on this in the next chapter).

If we take the two examples from the previous section, here are some things that the person may say to him or herself instead:

1. 'I'm feeling sad today, probably because I'm feeling a bit lonely and because my friends haven't been in touch for a while. It's pretty normal to feel like that from time to time; everyone probably does. It's not surprising I'm feeling low in energy; being a little lonely can make you feel like that sometimes. Actually, this has happened in the past, and I remember usually feeling better several hours later or the next day. I'm not going to dwell on it too much. Maybe I can just take it easy today and do something that feels nice to me. I don't have to push these feelings away; I can wait for them to pass and maybe soon things will feel different. I'm only human after all, and loneliness and sadness are just feelings that we experience from time to time. It doesn't mean anything serious; it just means I care about these things.'

2. 'Oh, here's my panic again. Hello panic! I know these feelings; I've had them lots of times. It doesn't feel nice, but I know it's not dangerous (remember the ideas from Chapter 2). It's just my body trying to tell me that I'm probably really anxious or stressed about something, or maybe something has been feeling a bit too much lately. I'm having these feelings because I'm human and I'm normal. It's actually a sign that things are working fine in my body. I wonder what's causing the stress for me. Hello dear panic, nice of you to pop up like this! Thank you for showing up and letting me know that maybe I need to slow down or relax somehow, or maybe focus my mind on calmer things. Yikes! It does feel strong. My body is really talking to me. It's okay, I know these feelings pass. Even if I do absolutely nothing at all, I know it all passes. It sure is intense being a human and teenager sometimes! I'm going to just wait until I feel a little better, but I know things always go back to normal eventually.'

My panic buddy

We invite you to create a panic buddy in your mind and/or on paper as one way of applying these acceptance strategies in a more playful way. This may represent all your panic and anxiety symptoms in the form of a little cartoon creature or a particular shape or object. It can be any size, shape, colour and texture. It can have facial features or simply be a blob or shape of some sort. What we ask is that you make it friendly. After all, your panic buddy is there trying to protect you in some way, even though it kind of gets it wrong quite often. So your panic buddy is actually a friend, and we encourage you to start to see your panic in this friendly, non-threatening way.

Your panic buddy is a bit like a very annoying but very well-meaning friend. Your panic buddy thinks that you need extra protection from danger, and it tells you to be on the lookout for things a lot of the time. It is scared of things and doesn't like to feel scared. It doesn't like to feel any difficult feelings. It wants to make sure that you don't do anything that will make the feelings worse. It keeps telling you things about your symptoms to make sure that you don't take your attention away and so that you don't forget your panic buddy.

So far you may have been responding to your panic buddy by trying very hard to push the panic buddy away. But it hasn't calmed the panic down, has it? We suggest that the panic buddy just needs a big hug and then perhaps needs to be placed in a corner somewhere until it gets bored. So for example, when you notice some panic symptoms, you could say, 'Hello, my little buddy, there you are. It's okay, thanks for popping up. You're very anxious right now, aren't you? But it's okay, we know what happens and we know nothing bad happens. I'm going to give you a little gentle squeeze and pop you over there. Panic is just a normal sensation. It means I'm alive and well! Now sit tight, little friend, we're doing just fine.'

Other approaches to try

Grounding and mindfulness

Once you get really good at noticing and accepting (and even embracing) your panic symptoms or panic buddy, you may want to practise some grounding or mindfulness strategies. You may have heard of these terms before. They basically refer to the ability to be in the present moment with your whole self. So making sure that you pay attention to all the parts of your body and all your senses rather than purely focusing on what's going on in your mind. We present an example of how this can be practised on the next page. This can have a very soothing and calming effect. When you are in the present moment with your whole self, your mind slows down, and your body becomes more still. Some people really like using their five senses in order to get themselves more in the present moment: sound, sight, taste, smell and touch.

Try this:

- Name three things you can hear right now.

- Name three things you can see in this moment.

- What can you taste in your mouth?

- What can you smell right now?

- Name three things that your body is connecting to right now (e.g., can you feel your feet on the ground? Can you feel your back or your sit bones against something? What do your clothes feel like against your skin?).

Applying silly and funny labels to feelings and thoughts

Another way of being more playful when dealing with difficult feelings or thoughts is to start giving them some humorous labels. It might not feel funny at first, but you might be surprised by how much an activity like this can take the 'fear' and 'terror' out of a situation. One client used to say to herself about her panic symptoms and fears of having a heart attack: 'Oh, there goes my *death-is-near* feeling again.' To her, that phrase just reminded her of how silly and unrealistic it was that she was really going to die, especially as she'd had hundreds of *death-is-near* feelings before, and it made her smile and feel better. We can't give you the labels to use, but we suggest you note down your main fears (e.g. I will collapse and embarrass myself totally) and then turn them into a one-word, silly label or short phrase (e.g. my *live-like-a-hermit-forever* feeling!).

Noticing the you within

We invite you to think a little more about this incredible idea that we as humans are able to observe our own thoughts and think about our own minds. It's like we are observing the workings of our minds from an *inner me* perspective. It supports the idea that *we are not our thoughts or our feelings*, but in fact could be connected to something greater that isn't limited by the workings of our mind and body. This is, of course, a theory and extremely difficult to prove, but it does sit at the centre of many faiths, and has received more recent support by scientists in the field of quantum physics. The important thing to remember is that there is a part of you, a *real you*, if you like, that can rise above your thoughts and feelings and can never be destroyed by any physical danger. Knowing this can be incredibly freeing and particularly useful for times when you feel overwhelmed with difficult emotions. It allows you to connect yourself to the moment and to realize that the *real you* can cope no matter what.

It might help to think about the *inner me* as a computer programmer and the physical experiences you have (including your thoughts and emotions) being part of a computer game. The programmer is independent of the game. They may be really good at playing it, but they can also step away from it. Likewise, rather than getting caught up in the 'game', you can take a step back and try to connect to the creator of the game.

Switching your awareness to the *real you* can be achieved through techniques known as *grounding*, and there are many practical ways this can be done. Some people choose to focus in on their feet on the ground or on a place deep within their belly or heart and say to themselves, 'No matter what, I am not my feelings or my thoughts. I can cope with this situation; I can stand firm until it passes.' Being able to connect with the deeper *you* in this way means that you will be much more able to be kind and compassionate towards yourself. We expand on these self-compassion ideas further in the next chapter.

Round up

We hope that you have reflected on how helpful it can be to notice, accept and even welcome and embrace difficult feelings and thoughts. We will always experience feelings, whether they are strong or weak, negative or positive, and if we can find ways to allow these to come and go, then we give up the struggle and battle and need to control them. This in turn helps us to feel calmer, more grounded and more able to cope in any situation.

Questions to get you thinking

1. *Do I try to control or push away my feelings, sensations or thoughts? How do I do this? Does it help me in the long run or make me feel worse?*

2. *What alternative responses in this chapter appeal to me? Which ones will I try first?*

Chapter 5

Being Your Own Personal Cheerleader

You've seen how becoming kinder and more friendly towards your panic symptoms and other difficult emotions can actually help to make you feel calmer and for the symptoms to subside more quickly. Now we are turning our focus towards how you can become kinder towards yourself. Some young people tend to be much kinder towards their friends and family than they are to themselves. From the hundreds of young people we have spoken with, it seems often that those young people who are sensitive, kind, understanding, accepting and generous towards others also sometimes seem to be pretty unkind towards and hard on themselves. It's like they use a different set of rules for others and see others in a much kinder way. So for example, they may see that their friend making a mistake in football practice is very understandable and no big deal. But when this happens to them, they tell themselves off and churn it over in their minds for a long time, thinking they really messed up and let the team down. Perhaps you have noticed this in people you know, or perhaps you can even recognize this in yourself?

Why do we give ourselves
such a hard time sometimes?

We don't know why this happens exactly. We know that as humans our brains are wired in a way that means we naturally want to fit in and be liked and accepted by others. You may recall some of the ways that our brains work from Chapter 2. Sometimes this can be related to a person's personality and other times it's to do with the messages that others have given them or things they have observed as they've grown up. Usually it's a combination of reasons. We will talk more about this further on in this chapter.

Knowing that your human brain
is wired a certain way and that's okay

If we lived in the forest like gorillas, from a survival point of view, our need to be accepted and not rejected from a group would probably mean that we would be more likely to stay within a tribe and our chance of survival from predators or other dangers would be better. So from an evolutionary point of view, our brains are naturally wired from thousands of years ago to tell us to 'do enough for the group', 'be as good or better than others', 'toe the line', 'try hard', 'do a good job' and 'be liked'. It's important to remind ourselves that the way our brains are designed is not perfect and there are certain tendencies that all humans have that were developed thousands of years ago in completely different living environments. So first of all, let's just accept this and keep reminding ourselves that we are sometimes working with outdated brain wiring!

What we hear from others

When growing up we are often told to 'do a good job', 'try our best', 'achieve good grades', 'be a good girl or boy' and so on. In addition to this, we are constantly faced with media and advertising and social media, full of messages about how we should look, what we should eat, the things we should own or the activities we should be doing. There is no end to all the 'shoulds', and most of these messages are rarely based on real people or real situations. For some individuals, these messages really stick and can make them feel like they need to be better and better all the time. We sometimes refer to this as someone having high standards. No matter what they achieve or manage to do, it feels not good enough for them and like they ought to have done better. In some ways this can help a person to achieve many things, and sometimes it can be a motivator for things like studying hard or practising a sport or musical instrument well or doing a good job. So it may lead to good grades or other achievements and can feel helpful or useful for a while. However, having high standards all the time, or trying to measure up to unreal expectations from, for example, the media, means that pretty soon it may start to feel impossible. All the achievements may start to feel not good enough, and this can have a negative impact on a person's mood, stress levels and their motivation. It starts to feel 'never good enough', and that kind of feeling is pretty demotivating.

Why is how you treat yourself important?

We are bringing up this very important topic because anxiety and panic symptoms often go hand in hand with feelings of having to be 'good enough' or with feelings of things being overwhelming due to very high standards and/or stress levels. We have put together a useful list of practical things that young people can do in order to manage their stress levels in general in Chapter 6. In this chapter, we want to give you some ideas about how you can reduce the harsh voice and stress that you may be putting on yourself in your mind. By finding a kinder voice to use towards yourself, you may find that having panic symptoms no longer feels so terrifying and the symptoms no longer have a hold over you. It may also make you more likely to be successful in applying the other ideas in this book and to be able to cope better with any setbacks in the future. In a more general sense, developing a kinder voice may mean you are more willing to pace yourself, be patient and not expect immediate results, which are all useful approaches in all sorts of life situations.

Self-compassion

Self-compassion is a term that is sometimes used to describe the act of being kind to yourself and 'treating yourself like a friend'. Learning this skill can help a person to stay calmer and more content and to experience more positive emotions on a regular basis. It involves developing a compassionate voice and language to use towards yourself. Imagine what a difference it could make to have a personal cheerleader encouraging you, rather than a bully inside your head.

Some examples of phrases such as these may be:

- I did alright.
- These symptoms will get better.
- I'm doing just fine.
- It's working out well.
- I did what I could in the situation.
- It's really okay to feel anxious.
- I'm learning all the time.
- Most people feel like this from time to time.
- With practice I can learn even more.
- My approach is a good one.
- I can do it my way.

- I've really had a go at this.
- Well done me.
- Keep it up.
- I like that I tried.
- It's been a tough day, time to relax.
- This will pass.
- I know I can handle it.
- I can always ask for help.
- My panic is not dangerous.
- I'm so proud of myself.
- I'm fine as I am.

Keeping an eye on your expectations and that 'little critic' within

You may have already got to know your panic buddy from Chapter 4. And we hope very much that you are becoming good friends, and you maybe give your panic buddy a bit of a hug or friendly poke from time to time (or you may be working towards this). In the same way, you may also have a little critic in your mind that tells you off for certain things and basically jumps on any tiny little thing that it thinks you may have done wrong. This little critic sits in most of us, and, again, it is part of being human. When it's tiny and we have a fairly friendly relationship with it, it can actually be helpful. Our little critic may say, 'You're cycling a bit fast and all over the road today. That's not great, you know.' And then we see a fast car coming around the bend, and we may think that our little critic helped us to be safe in that moment. But if our little critic is not so little, and if we have a difficult relationship with it, the critic can quickly take over our thoughts and feelings and make us feel pretty lousy.

> **Us:** I'm going to call my friend today.
>
> **Little critic:** What for? They might ignore you.
>
> **Us:** Do you think so? Maybe you're right. I don't know.
>
> **Little critic:** Of course I'm right, your friends often ignore you.
>
> **Us:** They do not. Go away and stop saying that. Well, sometimes they do.
>
> **Little critic:** Sounds like you can't even control what you're thinking. You can be a bit of a loser sometimes, you know.
>
> **Us:** I don't want to listen to you. This is so annoying. Maybe I am a loser.
>
> **Little critic:** Yeah, you better stay on the safe side and not call your friend.
>
> **Us:** Okay, they probably don't want to hear from me anyway.

You probably now know what we are going to suggest. That's right, go ahead and start making friends with your little critic as well. The more you just let him or her 'jabber on' and not take it too seriously, the less the little critic will bother you and the more you will be able to focus on achieving your goals and what you actually want to do.

Examples of alternative responses

You: Hello my little critic. I thought you might show up. We know each other well now. I know you're only trying to protect me and that actually you have my best interest in mind. But you often go overboard, don't you? It's okay. I'm glad you're there anyway, and I'm glad you're trying to protect me. But you sometimes get it wrong and exaggerate things. So I'm saying, 'Thanks for showing up.' 'Thanks but no thanks.' I'm giving you a little virtual hug, and then I'm going to listen to what I want to do instead. And what I want to do is call my friend, so here goes...

Little critic: Well, okay, I did warn you, but maybe you're right. I'll come back later.

Not letting your thoughts take you for a ride

Another way not to engage with your little critic too much is to be mindful not to 'hold on' to unhelpful thoughts for too long. What we mean by this is that sometimes when a thought pops into our mind, for example 'My friends don't really like me', we can latch on to it for too long and be taken for a bit of an unpleasant, rough ride. The reason it can be unpleasant is if we hold on to this type of thought, it usually gets bigger and attracts more thoughts that are similar (e.g. 'Even my sister doesn't really like me', 'No one cares about me', 'I'm horrible').

Imagine for a moment that thoughts are just like cars going by as you stand on the side of a road. Some are nice looking, some are rusty and beaten up, some are moving fast, some slow. If you grab on to the bumper of one of these cars, you are going to be dragged behind it. So if you notice some unpleasant or critical thoughts zoom by, instead of grabbing on to the bumper and being taken on a bumpy ride, simply let the thought zoom by. You can also just notice what type of thought it is, like you would if you noticed that a car was 'red' or 'really fast'. For example, 'Gosh, that was a pretty negative thought I just had. Oh well, I'll let it go for now...'

Comparing yourself with others

This section will be very short. Just don't do it! Every human being is an individual, and there are no two people exactly alike, or even close to alike. Therefore, how can we even begin to compare ourselves to each other? It's pointless, because it's like comparing poodles with Dobermans; they're just different. We don't say, 'Gosh that poodle looks nothing like that Doberman. There must be something wrong with it.' Okay, this is a silly example, but hopefully it demonstrates that making comparisons between different things or different individuals is meaningless and it usually devalues one of the things being compared. Instead, we really want to encourage you to start being in the habit of rejoicing in your individuality. This is a really genuine way of being very kind to yourself.

Rejoicing in being yourself and in your mistakes!

Think about some of the most famous and positively influential people in human history such as Gandhi or Nelson Mandela. Did they tend to do things just like others and try to fit in with what others were saying or thinking? Definitely not. They spoke their own truth, stood their ground and were not ashamed to make every bit of their individuality known to others. This takes courage. But we believe that this type of courage can be found in every young person. Yes, in you too. We are not saying you need to go out there and change the world (although you may want to), but we are saying go out there and be your very true, unapologetic self, and go ahead and make lots of 'mistakes'. It is these so-called mistakes that often lead to the most interesting experiences, profound learning and developments and amazing advancements. Yes, you may encounter a few foolish people on the way, who judge you on whether you are like them or other people they know, but perhaps those people just haven't realized their mistake yet and still have some learning to do too!

Connecting with others and with what is important

Finally, we wanted to mention that connecting with people you value and with what is important to you is another authentic way of being kind to yourself. Make some time to think about the people in your life who make you feel good or who you learn the most from. Or you may want to think about the type of people you want to have more connection with in the future. Now think about the activities and issues that are really important to you. For example, are you someone who really values kindness to animals, or are you interested in particular sports or music or in world issues such as pollution? Make a list of all the things that matter to you and that you value. Once you have a clearer picture of the people who matter to you and the issues that are important to you, make an effort to spend more time connecting with these things. In this way what you are ultimately saying to yourself is: 'What I like and what is important to me really matters. I'm going to invest my time in this because I matter and I value myself.' It can feel really strange when you first start to do this. Some may even worry that they are being conceited or selfish by not doing what others want them to do. The more you try it, though, the more confident and comfortable you will feel about being yourself, and that will really help you as you progress to the ideas we will talk about in Chapters 7 and 8 – so try not to skip over this and give it a proper go.

Start small

Many young people tell us that being kind to themselves, or self-compassion, is the hardest thing to put into practice in a genuine way. It feels 'weak' somehow and a bit 'wishy washy' and even silly at times. Others have told us that it's downright embarrassing and completely uncomfortable to 'be kind to myself'. We understand that this may not be easy, especially if you are someone who has been saying critical things to yourself for a long time. It might feel really unnatural to begin with. We encourage you not to throw this idea away completely, however. If you can master this skill in an authentic way, it will continue to nourish and help you for the rest of your life. Many adults find this difficult as well, and they sometimes say that they wish they had learnt to do this when they were younger. Ultimately, the more you value yourself, the more you will be able to value, encourage and support others.

So start out small and see how you go. When you catch yourself about to say, 'I've really messed up', stop and think how you would speak about the situation to someone you cared about very much. Then say this to yourself and get on with the rest of your day. Over time you may find that your little critic is not so critical any more and is starting to fade into the background. You may develop a kind voice that naturally jumps to your defence when the little critic has something to say.

Round up

Being kind to yourself or practising self-compassion can be challenging, but it is an incredibly worthwhile and effective practice that will allow you to reap many rewards now and in the future. It helps us to accept ourselves no matter what we are experiencing and to talk to ourselves with kindness, love and understanding. These approaches in turn create a foundation whereby panic symptoms and anxiety no longer have a hold on us in any situation.

Questions to get you thinking

1. *Do you have an inner little critic that sometimes beats you up too much? What do you tend to say to yourself?*

2. *What are some ways that you can start to be kinder to yourself?*

3. *What's important to you?*

4. *What are some of the things you can start saying to yourself in a kinder way? Jot down a few ideas of things that may sound okay to you when you say them to yourself.*

Chapter 6
Helping to Restore Your Body's Natural Balance

We hope you have found some of the ideas and suggestions given so far interesting and helpful. Perhaps you have discovered a little bit more about why your panic symptoms appear and seem to take over, and you may have already made a start on trying to accept and embrace your feelings and be more understanding towards yourself. If you have, you are on the right track to make some more new discoveries and to plan your steps to freedom, which you will learn more about in Chapters 7 and 8.

It may be, however, that you have found some or many of the ideas quite challenging, and possibly even daunting. Perhaps what you have read has made you feel uncomfortable, or you think what we are asking you to do is strange and might not work for you. Certainly, if you have experienced panic symptoms for a long time, it would not be unusual for you to recognize the habits and cycles discussed in the previous chapters and want to do something to change them but feel overwhelmed and stuck when the time comes. If this is something that you have felt, or suspect will happen when you give things a try, then please know that this chapter was written especially with you in mind.

One of the greatest barriers to making positive changes is the pressure we put on ourselves.

As you will have just read in the previous chapter, it is hugely important to develop self-compassion so that we don't make things even harder for ourselves when we face challenges, but this is in itself a tricky skill to develop. If and when you experience setbacks as you work your way through the remaining ideas, you may feel like you are failing and become deflated. We have seen this happen many times in our work. So for now, instead of focusing on how to find freedom from panic, we would like to offer you an entirely different goal: to increase your body's natural state of calm and to restore your balance.

Whenever you start to feel overwhelmed or have done something draining, take a break from panic (and thinking about ways in which you can overcome it) and instead take a moment to consider the importance of rest and how you may be able to incorporate it into your daily life.

'Rest and digest' – the natural state of calm

Up until now, we have talked a lot about our 'fight or flight' response and how it becomes activated during times of stress or perceived danger. You now know that this evolved as a survival mechanism to help you react quickly in life-threatening situations. It is relevant to you because your panic symptoms are part of this biological reaction. It is as important, though, to remember that our body works best when it is in its more natural state of 'rest and digest'. This state allows our body to slow down and undertake all the necessary jobs to ensure we remain well. When we aren't in any danger, our body can get on with the task of functioning well and simply 'being'.

The slow and gentle physical responses activated during 'rest and digest' are the exact opposite to those activated during episodes of panic. When all is safe and well, blood pressure is lower; breathing is slower, deeper and more regular; our food digested; and toxins and waste are removed properly.

Something that may seem obvious, but is often forgotten, is that it is impossible to be in 'fight or flight' and 'rest and digest' at the same time. As well as feeling incredibly uncomfortable, if we spend too much time living in a body responding to fear, our body doesn't get the chance to do what it is meant to, and we can start to experience a whole range of additional health problems and unpleasant symptoms on top of our panic experiences (e.g. tiredness, stomach aches, constipation, headaches and mood swings). When this happens, it's really no wonder that everything can feel overwhelming. If we begin to understand that these symptoms are our body's way of letting us know that it needs more rest, we can start to do things to restore the balance and counteract the negative fallout from all the stress and cope better with a whole range of situations.

Although humans can and do enter a state of panic very quickly, there is another alternative way of existing that needs to be activated in order to restore balance to our nervous systems and help us to confront challenges.

Deep breathing

The quickest and easiest way to enter 'rest and digest' mode is to change your breathing. Deep breathing slows everything down and signals to your body that you are safe and that it is okay to relax.

Since your body cannot be in two modes at once (alert and calm), the more you practise deep breathing, the calmer your body will become.

You can do slow, deep breathing by breathing in through your nose for a count of four, holding your breath for a count of seven and slowly pushing your breath back out and emptying your lungs fully for a count of eight.

It is best to practise this regularly and when you have the opportunity to get yourself comfortable. Once you get really good at it, you may try to slow down your breathing before and after more challenging experiences. It is best not to use this practice when experiencing panic symptoms, because it can easily become a panic trap and a way of controlling panic, as discussed in Chapter 3.

Below is an exercise that should only take a few minutes and is a great activity to promote a general sense of relaxation. If you get into the habit of doing deep breathing as part of your daily routine (e.g., when you get into bed at night), you will help to restore and balance your nervous system and you can expect to feel calmer and more energized over time.

A deep breathing exercise

Find a quiet space and position yourself in a comfortable position with a straight spine (such as sitting upright in a chair or lying down on your back).

1. *Close your eyes or look down to a soft gaze to remove distraction and assist in inward focus.*

2. *Start to notice the movements of your breath. (Are you breathing in and out from your chest in an even manner? Are you breathing rapidly or slowly?)*

3. Scan your body and release any tension held. (Let your shoulders relax, your arms fall to your side and release your stomach muscles.)

4. Begin to breathe with intention. Inhaling deeply and slowly through your nose, feeling your centre expand as you fill your body with the breath. Gradually exhale out through your mouth, letting all of the stale air out.

5. Notice how your body rises and falls with each breath you take, and with each exhalation imagine your body releasing stress and tension.

6. Repeat for ten cycles of breath.

7. Take a few moments to notice how you feel physically, mentally and emotionally.

If you are having trouble noticing the rise and fall of your body, it may be helpful to place your hands on your belly or ribcage. Your hands should be gently lifting as you fill your lungs with air and then lowering with each out breath.

It is possible that focusing on your breath may initially increase your panic symptoms. If this happens or the exercise simply makes you feel more nervous, you could try taking only a few deep breaths and gradually working your way up to more. If you find that you really don't like doing this or find it too difficult, you don't have to persist - in fact, you don't need to give any of it a go. There are other things you can try instead. We suggest reading all the suggestions in this chapter first, and then selecting the ones that appeal the most to you.

Muscle relaxation

Another relatively easy but effective way of keeping your body relaxed is to regularly release built-up muscle tension and stiffness formed in the body. Yoga achieves this through the stretching and lengthening of muscle groups, and it helps restore a sense of balance and calm, particularly if you do it on a regular basis with the help of an instructor to support and guide your movement and postures. Yoga also provides a more active way of 'being in the moment' and 'being with your whole self', as introduced in Chapter 4.

We won't go through specific yoga stretches here, but due to an increase in its popularity and the recognition of its benefit on physical and mental health, it is relatively easy to find yoga classes to join throughout the UK. We recommend finding a certified yoga practitioner if you want to learn more about how you can benefit.

If yoga isn't something you want to try just yet, an alternative and safe exercise for you to do on your own is progressive muscle relaxation (PMR).

This involves systematically squeezing and then releasing each of the muscle groups in your body, increasing your awareness of built-up tension and, more importantly, helping you to let go of stress.

If you want to have a go at trying it, we have included a basic exercise for you to follow on the next page.

Before you try PMR, don't be alarmed if things feel a little sore to begin with. It is very common for our muscles to stiffen without us noticing, and, if and when you first try PMR, you may find that your body is more rigid than you expected. If this is the case, then as well as doing the exercise more regularly, you may want to consider setting yourself reminders to check in on your muscles and to make adjustments to your posture throughout the day.

The positive effects of relaxing your muscles are usually felt almost immediately; however, like deep breathing, we encourage you to include the exercise below as part of a daily routine in order to increase your awareness of what it feels like to relax and to really enjoy the benefits in the longer term.

Progressive muscle relaxation exercise

Get comfortable. (You don't need to be in a quiet place or lying down for PMR.)

1. *Focus on your breathing and start simple, deep breathing (see previous exercise).*

2. *Starting with your feet, tighten and release your muscles. Clench your toes and press your heels towards the ground. Squeeze tightly for a few breaths, and then release. Now flex your feet in, pointing your toes up towards your head. Hold for a few seconds and then release.*

3. *Continue to work your way up your body, tightening and releasing each muscle group. Work your way up in this order: legs, glutes, abdomen, back, hands, arms, shoulders, neck and face. Try to tighten each muscle group for a few breaths and then slowly release. Repeat any areas that feel especially stiff.*

4. *Take a few moments to notice how you feel physically, mentally and emotionally.*

Visualization

Unsurprisingly, even when we are purposefully trying to relax, our mind often messes it up for us. As we have said, our thoughts and the images we create have a powerful influence over our physical responses. If we happen to have a worrisome thought and start to imagine a worst-case scenario, our body will automatically start preparing for danger and quickly ruin our chance of reaching a peaceful state.

Just as our imagination can be a great source of stress, it can, however, also be used to help us unwind. Visualization involves focusing your mind on calming mental images and, with practice, you can achieve a more relaxed state of mind.

The scene that you imagine can be anywhere that brings you a sense of wellbeing – it may be a place you hold in your memory or a fantasy. Use your creativity and experiment with exploring different places in your mind. One day you may imagine lying down in a large field of wildflowers; another day you may find yourself enjoying a beautiful view from a mountain or perhaps you find yourself exploring an ancient forest whilst riding bareback on a stunning unicorn, accompanied by a friendly troll named Wilbert. Anything is possible.

When visualizing a scene, it is important to try to really imagine yourself in the environment and experience it through all your senses, rather than looking down on it or watching it from afar. For example, if you visualize yourself on a white sandy beach, try to ask yourself: what colour is the water? What do the lapping waves sound like? How does the sand feel under my feet? What can I smell? What does the air taste like? Imagine all the different sights, sounds, smells and textures associated with these varying places.

If you find yourself becoming easily distracted or if you find it difficult to fully emerge yourself into your fantasy, you may find it helpful to search the Internet or your local library for some 'guided visualization' recordings in the first instance. However, as with all the techniques discussed, the more often you practise, the more natural it will become and the quicker you will find yourself being able to enjoy a state of relaxation.

Simple meditation

Many people have heard of the benefits of meditation. Meditation does not need to be complex, and it doesn't always require as much effort as you may think.

A very basic meditation simply involves you focusing on one thing for a short length of time and noticing when your mind wanders so you can gently bring it back to the object of your focus.

The idea is that you become better at learning how to enjoy being in the current moment and give your body a break from the stream of thoughts that come up. It will also help you with not letting your thoughts take you for a ride, as discussed in Chapter 4.

It is up to you how long you want to try meditating and what you want to focus on, but below are some ideas to get you started. You may not become a Buddhist monk overnight, but with practice, you may well find a little bit of zen you never knew you needed.

Possible meditation focus

The sound of a fan or buzzing of the fridge in the background.

The flame of a candle.

The sensation of an ice cube on your hand.

The sensation of grass on your bare feet.

Relaxing pursuits

Whilst the above strategies are best achieved when still, being inactive (such as sitting on the sofa or lying on your bed) is not the same as relaxing. In fact, when we do 'nothing', our minds often bombard us with negative thoughts, making it harder both to relax and to find motivation to do anything that would be more helpful.

For example, you may spend many hours on the sofa appearing to be 'relaxing'; however, if you have an assignment due and you are avoiding working on it, you may experience waves of anxiety as you occasionally remember the looming task and everything you still have to get done. Similarly, scrolling on your phone may seem a relatively carefree activity; however, depending on what you read, you may expose yourself to some pretty negative material.

In order to achieve more genuine states of relaxation, it is important to do things that bring you a sense of fulfilment and happiness.

This may seem indulgent or trivial in comparison to doing things that need to be achieved; however, if your week is filled with stress and less-than-rewarding activities, it is even more essential that you make relaxing pursuits a priority.

The things that bring us happiness and balance out more challenging times are different for each of us. One of the mistakes people often make is copying what others enjoy, without really giving thought to whether or not the activity is bringing about a sense of personal happiness and wellbeing. Another challenge in that many of us don't really know what we enjoy. If this is you, try to let go of any particular expectations you may have about certain hobbies (and particularly any idea that you have to be 'good' at something) and instead experiment with trying new things.

It can be helpful to try to remember what it was you liked to do in your younger years and to recreate that sense of playfulness and creativity that often gets pushed aside as we become older.

Below is a list of some things to get you started as you think about what you may want to try as a relaxing pursuit. Remember, the aim is not to become good at something, but to prioritize and give yourself permission to spend your time on things that give you pleasure and calm your nervous system.

Activities to try

- Painting
- Modelling
- Dressing up
- Baking
- Cooking
- Woodwork
- Flower arranging
- Photography
- Colouring
- Gardening
- Volunteering at an animal shelter

- Writing
- Dancing
- Drama
- Jogging
- Weightlifting
- Helping neighbours or in the local community

- Writing computer programs
- Collecting things
- Poetry
- Fundraising
- Conservation projects

The benefit of nature

Another easy and wonderful way to recharge your body and clear your mind is to step out into nature. Like all animals, we are genetically programmed to find nature interesting, and when we begin to focus on trees, plants and water, we often find they have a calming effect on us. Unfortunately, our busy schedules and tendency to rush from one place to another means that we often forget to look up and connect with our surroundings.

Instead of treating the outdoors as simply being a way of 'getting somewhere', make a plan to go on a walk with the intention of noticing the natural wonders of our planet.

Go ahead and challenge yourself to spot life happening all around you and enjoy the feeling of serenity that comes from observing the nature. Comfort can be gained from watching a leaf fall, birds bathing or buds blossoming. When you see life flowing naturally from one season to the next without any pressure, you just may start to believe it's possible for you too. And if and when this happens, take a moment to enjoy a deep breath and embrace any new insights that come to you.

In addition to simply quieting our minds, the airborne chemicals produced by trees and the negative ions generated in natural surfaces (such as soil, rocks and water) can also help to restore general wellbeing in our bodies. By simply increasing the amount of time you spend in nature and by making direct physical contact with the earth, you can absorb the earth's positive energetic properties.

This has a proven impact on your body and has been found to lower your production of cortisol (the stress hormone), reduce your blood pressure and increase antioxidants that help to fight disease.

Whenever your bare feet or skin comes into contact with the earth, free electrons are directly taken up into the body.

With this in mind, why not follow in the footsteps of our ancestors and physically connect with nature? It may sound too good to be true, but don't knock it until you've tried it.

Ways to physically connect with nature

- Go to the woods.
- Walk barefoot.
- Swim in open waters.
- Grow vegetables.
- Lie down in the shade of a tree.
- Build a treehouse.
- Do some woodwork.
- Polish some pebbles.
- Pick wildflowers.
- Roll down a hill.

- Collect firewood.
- Throw stones at a target.
- Go jogging in the rain.
- Make an animal shelter.
- Hug a tree.
- Build a den out of sticks and leaves.
- Spend time with animals outside.
- Hold and feel stones or crystals in your hands.
- Visit some farmland.
- Have a picnic in the park.
- Care for a potted plant.
- Plant some seeds.
- Splash in a stream.
- Jump barefoot in a mud puddle.
- Mould something out of some mud.

A comforting touch

As soon as we enter the world, we rely on a caregiver's touch to provide security and a sense of safety. When we see another human or animal in pain, most of us recognize the natural pull to step closer in order to offer a stroke, hug or physical reassurance.

For most of us, the feeling of gentle pressure against our skin is a pleasant experience and, without realizing it, our heart rate and blood pressure naturally come down.

You will know for yourself whether you are someone who may benefit from touch and how it makes you feel. If you have experienced sexual or physical abuse or are sensitive to touch, then you may find that human touch triggers your 'fight or flight' responses rather than building your experience of calm and security. If this is the case, our advice is to only attempt what feels comfortable (if anything) and experiment with ways in which you can increase the benefits of touch, with or without the need for physical contact with anyone else. And of course, if you find yourself restricted as to whether you can make contact with others (e.g., when social distancing measures are in place or you don't have anyone you would feel comfortable enough in asking), then take a look at some of the alternative options below.

Touch can come in many forms, and coming up with creative ways that you can experience firm but gentle contact against your skin will increase your moments of balance and sense of security.

To help you get started, here are some easy ways to receive comforting touch (with or without the need for another person to be involved):

- Giving or receiving a foot massage
- Giving or receiving a head massage
- Stroking a pet
- Giving or receiving a bear hug
- Giving or receiving a firm handshake
- Massaging your own hand
- Briskly walking (try with or without shoes!)
- Wrapping yourself in a weighted blanket
- Rubbing your arms and legs and torso
- Tapping your forehead and temples
- Pushing your palms up against a wall
- Trying some yoga poses
- Investing in a neck massager
- Feeling the surface beneath your feet (e.g. grass, pebbles)

A note on caffeine and unhelpful foods

Since we are discussing ways in which you can support your body to enter its natural state of 'rest and digest', it is worth mentioning the negative effect caffeinated drinks and certain foods can have on this.

Some foods and drinks may be more likely to trigger and prolong the body's 'fight or flight' responses, as well as causing mood changes and other unhelpful physiological reactions.

We do not suggest cutting these foods out entirely; in fact, sudden changes to your diet are not recommended and could really upset your natural balance. However, you may wish to experiment with reducing their consumption and seeing if it helps you to feel calmer. If you notice a positive difference, you should seek further advice and support from your GP and a nutritionist who can offer you a better understanding of why these foods are not good for your wellbeing and the kind of diet that could help you.

Foods and drinks that may be unhelpful for some individuals

- Caffeine – found in coffee, black teas and common soda drinks

- Artificial and refined sugars – these hide in all sorts of food. Take a look at food labels to see if what you are eating has them. What you find may surprise you!

- Gluten

- Processed foods

- Foods containing a lot of preservatives and/or colourings

- Alcohol

- Any mind-altering substances

- Dairy products

- Fried food

- Fat-free foods, which may be high in sodium

- High-meat diet

If you find the idea of being more relaxed and calm inviting and would like to give the strategies in this chapter a go, you will achieve this more easily if your body is fed and nourished well.

Round up

During episodes of high stress and challenge, our body is in 'fight or flight' mode and is working hard to keep us safe. This is not an ideal state of functioning and can make everything seem overwhelming and difficult. There are lots of simple but effective ways in which we can help our bodies to decrease the time we spend in the 'fight or flight' response by enjoying more time in our natural 'rest and digest' state. If you try some of the previous suggestions on a regular basis, we are confident that you will experience improvements in mood and your overall wellbeing – and it will make it much easier for you to let go and release yourself from your panic traps too.

Questions to get you thinking

1. *When could you try deep breathing and/or PMR?*

2. *How often do you do something that makes you happy? What could you try out this week?*

3. *Where is your nearest park or nature trail? How long would it take to get there?*

4. *The natural world has much to teach us about the simplicity of life. What is happening in the natural world? What will the next season bring?*

5. *When was the last time you found yourself relaxing? How long did it last?*

Chapter 7
Making New Discoveries

We hope that you have enjoyed reading Chapters 4, 5 and 6.
Accepting and even embracing panic symptoms is a great, albeit
difficult, skill to learn that you can use whilst also trying out some of
the ideas included in the next two chapters. Being kind to yourself is
going to be key if you want to put into practice the ideas that follow.
You will also be activating your threat system a lot, and so being able
to self-soothe and be in the 'rest and digest' state is really important.
Those skills may in themselves be enough for you to feel you are
becoming free from your panic and that it is not such a problem any
more. However, you may feel that you need to challenge yourself a
little more to truly feel that your panic is no longer controlling your
life and getting in the way.

   This chapter and the next will help you do this. We are going to
introduce some ideas that may help you to change the way you think
and behave in response to your panic symptoms. These in turn will
help to reduce your feelings of anxiety or panic.

   In this chapter, we are going to talk about how you can

challenge some of your anxious thoughts/interpretations about panic. Sometimes, accepting or embracing your panic symptoms can be hard, especially if you truly believe that they are dangerous or that you will not be able to cope with them. We are going to help you question those beliefs and hopefully gather new information to challenge them. We will do this by getting you to design and try out some experiments.

Experiments help you to make new discoveries.

We use experiments a lot in psychological therapy. They are not dissimilar to scientific experiments. The goal is the same: to test out our predictions or hypotheses to see if something happens or not or whether something is definitely true. So for example, in a science experiment, we may decide to mix two chemicals together, and predict what happens: does the colour change, is there a reaction, does the consistency change? This helps us to learn about the properties of these substances and their reactions. The same is true for psychological experiments. We want to test out what happens if we behave in a certain way: if I stand in a room with a spider, will it run towards me and scurry up my leg, or might it run away?

Being willing to give it a go

We are hoping that, as you have got this far in our book, you are willing to try a few new things to gain freedom from your panic problems and you have already started doing so. We are now going to challenge you a bit more and ask you to actually face your fears head on. You may be feeling nervous about doing this, which is completely understandable. You will probably have heard this term and know that this involves doing the very things that make you feel anxious, for example people with a fear of spiders being asked to have a spider crawl on their hand. We are confident that by actually facing your fears you will be able to change some of your thoughts or interpretations about panic as well as some of your behaviours, which will in turn lead you to feel less anxious or panicked. So, yes, we are going to ask you to try some things that mean facing your panic symptoms head on (even purposely making them happen) by using the experiments we describe in this chapter (and by creating a gradual plan in the next one). It might be scary to start with, but remember all those skills you have learnt and begun to use from the book so far. Try to accept and embrace those feelings; keep an eye out for your panic buddy. Notice your inner critic and remind yourself what you would say to a friend. Allow time to rest and digest. You are definitely at the right point to give these new challenges a go.

Why do an experiment?

The main purpose of conducting an experiment is to get some hard evidence: does my anxious thought or interpretation come true or not? This is really important. It is very hard to just try to convince ourselves that the thought either won't come true or isn't true. You hopefully will have written down your anxious thoughts or interpretations about your panic symptoms in Chapter 3. Have a look back at them.

We really want to be able to simply notice these thoughts and say, 'Oh, that's my panic buddy again' (as we talked about in Chapter 4). However, sometimes the thoughts are too scary and powerful, and you may not feel confident in knocking them back. Reducing their power a bit by gathering evidence can really help. After all, if you have information that tells you that your panic buddy is talking nonsense when they pop up again, it's far easier to say, 'You know what, I am just going to say hi to my panic buddy and not engage with them.'

We also talked in Chapter 2 about our attentional bias, where our brain tends to focus on the evidence that suggests our thought is true and misses other pieces of information. This makes it even harder to sit with these thoughts.

Experiments allow us to override our attentional bias and gather alternative evidence. Since we already know we are prone to making mistakes and jumping to negative conclusions when we are feeling anxious, it is always a good idea to test everything out properly. Remember, that's what your neocortex is for!

But I thought I was supposed to do less or do nothing about my panic?

Hang on a minute! You might be thinking that on the one hand we are telling you to do less about your panic, to 'do nothing', but on the other hand we are encouraging you to face things and 'do more'. Well, just to clarify, we hope you can see that 'doing less' and 'doing nothing' to try to control your panic can be very helpful, as this gets us out of panic traps and stops those panic cycles from getting worse. However, we are definitely not encouraging you to sit on your sofa and do nothing in general or to hide away from situations at home. We want you to do less about your panic symptoms so that you can do more of the important and fun stuff in your life. Since these things may not come naturally to you right now, it may require a little bit of effort to get things going again. But once you get started, we assure you, you'll find it far easier to live your life this way compared to one where you are trapped by panic.

Do less in response to your panic and do more in your life.

Getting started

What anxious thought or interpretation are you going to test out first?

What do you think will happen when you get your panic symptoms? What do they mean? Having a clear sense of this is likely to make the experiment much more useful.

Here are some examples from young people we have worked with:

- They are a sign that I am having a heart attack.

- I can't breathe; I might die.

- I might faint.

- They mean I am seriously ill or mad.

- I will lose control (and might do something awful or embarrassing).

- They won't stop and will last forever.

Here are a few more:

- If I don't try to stop my panic attack, it will go on forever and get worse.

- I have to control it, otherwise something bad will happen.

- I won't be able to cope if it happens again.

- At the first sign of any funny feelings, I need to get control of them.

- When I feel panicky, I need to sip some water and sit down or else it will get much worse.

- I need to carry my phone with me or I might panic and not be able to cope.

- I'm not going to be able to eat. I won't get enough food in me; my throat is shrinking.

You may have noted some down in Chapter 3 too; if so, jot them down again here:

1. ....

2. ....

3. ....

4. ....

Pick one to test out.

You may notice that your thoughts often come up as questions rather than statements. With anxiety, it is very common to have 'what if' thoughts, and of course the problem is that a question is hypothetical and you can't test it out. Your reptilian brain doesn't register these thoughts as questions. It just turns them straight into facts to avoid taking any risks. Go ahead and turn your questions into statements too. Not only will this make it easier to devise your experiments, but sometimes even seeing your thoughts written down in this way will make you have some doubts about them.

Make sure you're using a statement for this experiment; if your thought is a question, try to turn it into a statement. For example, 'What if I faint?' would turn into – 'I will faint'.

What does your experiment involve?

We now need to design an experiment that specifically tests this out. And, yes, you are right, this means you are inevitably going to have to experience your panic sensations to test out your thoughts. You may be wondering how on earth you can do this, as your physical symptoms tend to come out of the blue or only in particular situations or places. Here are some ways of doing this:

Wait for the sensations to arise and let them pass

One of the easiest ways to do this experiment is just to wait until your panic symptoms start. You may be thinking that you do this anyway, so this is not going to provide any new information. But the key is what you do in response to those sensations. Think about what you do at the moment: what are your panic traps? You may have noted these down in Chapter 3. We don't want you to do any of these things. We want you to 'sit with' the panic, observe it and see what happens - say hi to your panic buddy when they pop up. Remember what they look like, what sort of character they are, but don't try to get rid of them.

Try to sit with your panic symptoms - trying to get rid of them will make them worse

However, if it is too difficult or uncomfortable to simply sit with the panic and notice what happens, you can try a grounding exercise (like we talked about in Chapter 5, or refer to the websites at the end of the book). These are based on mindfulness and the concept of being in and noticing the moment. Timing is also important. Doing this when you are already feeling stressed is not going to work well. Do something relaxing beforehand - pick an activity from the last chapter perhaps. Plan to do something calming when you have completed the experiment.

Actively induce panic symptoms

Alternatively, you can actively induce physical sensations similar to panic ones. These experiments can be particularly powerful in challenging the idea that panic symptoms are harmful. Can they really be harmful if you can simply bring on these sensations yourself?

Here are some exercises (and the physical feelings they induce) that you can use to do just this:

Exercises	Physical feelings
Shake your head from side to side for 30 seconds	dizziness, nausea, unsteady on feet
Run on the spot as fast as you can for 1 minute	breathlessness, dizziness, fast heartbeat, feeling hot
Spin in a chair quickly for 1 minute	dizziness, nausea
Breathe through a straw for 2 minutes whilst squeezing your nostrils together	dizziness, breathlessness
Hold your breath for 30 seconds	dizziness, fast heartbeat
Breathe in and out very quickly for 1 minute	breathlessness, dizziness
Place your head between your knees for 30 seconds and then lift your head up to your normal position very quickly	dizziness, nausea

Read the list of panic symptoms in Chapter 1 slowly and imagine having the symptoms for a few minutes.

Think about the physical sensations you experience during panic episodes and identify which activities fit best with these. You may want to ask a friend or family member to have a go first so you can see what sensations they experience when doing one of these exercises. You can then pick one or more that best fit with your symptoms.

Again, we want you to let these symptoms pass without trying

to use any of your panic traps. Sit with them, let them rise and fall –
say hi to your panic buddy. Get a friend or family member to do this
with you. Compare symptoms and talk about them. If you can do
this, it is likely that you will notice and learn that these sensations
are not harmful. You are also likely to learn that they will go away on
their own.

How likely is it that your anxious thought will come true?

Next, rate how likely you think it is that your thought/interpretation
will actually happen. So you can think, 'If I feel breathless, how likely
is it that I will collapse or die?' You can give a number anywhere
between 0 and 100.

Have a go!

You may feel too anxious to actively induce your panic sensations;
many people do. Why would you want to induce these symptoms
when they are so awful? Remind yourself that the reason you are
doing this is to take the fear out of these sensations, to help you
realize that, despite feeling very unpleasant, they *won't* harm you
or kill you and they will go away. And they will go away quicker if you
don't try to control them or get rid of them. Nevertheless, these types
of exercises may be too hard for you, and that is okay. Be on the
lookout for your little critic. If you can't do it, think about what you
would say to a friend in a similar position, and say that to yourself.

What did you learn?

The big question is, what did you learn? You may be tempted to think,
'Phew, I am glad that is over. I am not going to think about it!' Don't!
It is really important that your brain processes this new information
so that you can store it in your memory for future experiences.
The best way of doing this is to record your experiment using the
questions here. Complete the first three questions before you do the

experiment and then come back and answer the last two when you have completed it.

1. What is my experiment? What am I going to do?

....

....

2. What thought am I testing out? What do I think will happen?

....

....

3. How likely is it that it will happen?

....

....

4. What actually happened? Was it as I predicted or different?

....

....

5. What have I learnt?

....

....

It is possible your thought did come true (e.g., 'I felt faint'). Although that may be disappointing, it is still useful information. Did all your predictions come true? ('No, I felt faint but I did not actually faint.') Did you cope with feeling faint? ('Yes, I did actually. It wasn't very nice, but I managed it.') Did it last for a long time? ('No, actually the faint feeling went away fairly quickly.')

Importantly, did you notice anything different about your panic symptoms when you decided to drop your panic traps? We have seen that over time, people start to notice that their panic symptoms seem to feel less severe and go away more quickly when they don't try as hard to control them or stop trying to control them altogether. Keep experimenting to see if this is perhaps true for you.

Panic symptoms are less severe or go away more quickly if you don't try to control them.

Restore the balance

If you have managed to carry out an experiment, you will have definitely activated your threat system. Now is a good time to restore the balance by engaging in a calming and self-soothing activity. Revisit Chapter 6 and have a go at one of the suggestions. Now might also be a good time to reward yourself. Acknowledge your efforts in some way.

Round up

Experiments are a great way of challenging your anxious thoughts and interpretations about your panic symptoms. They are hard work and can be quite scary to start with. But try an experiment, perhaps enlist the help of a friend or family member and record what you have done.

Questions to get you thinking

1. *Are you willing to put in that extra effort to overcome this, despite*

the fact it may be pretty scary? What might help you push yourself
to give it a go?

2. What anxious thoughts or fears would you really like to test out?

3. Who could you ask to help you?

4. What panic traps might you be tempted to use? Keep a lookout and
try to resist!

5. What do you hope to learn from this experiment?

6. Are there any times you have done this already, even if by accident?
What did you learn?

Chapter 8
Your Steps Towards Freedom

We hope that you have been able to design and perhaps conduct an experiment - or maybe several - to learn more about your panic symptoms. If so, well done! That is a massive achievement. You might remember that in Chapter 3 we talked about how lots of young people with panic symptoms avoid situations where they have experienced these unpleasant feelings or use panic traps to try to control the feelings. Inevitably, these young people begin to miss out on things, and their panic starts to get in the way of their everyday life. It also starts to chip away at their confidence and independence and sometimes even has negative effects on their self-esteem. We are going to talk more about this and will give you some ideas about how to tackle it so you can begin to fully re-engage in life.

What type of situations trigger panic symptoms?

Many young people feel that their panic symptoms have an enormous impact on their lives. They begin to notice that they avoid more and more situations where they have previously had panicky sensations. They might also begin to avoid situations that induce similar physical feelings, such as sport or running up a hill or up the stairs. Often young people notice that they are beginning to avoid particular types of situations, such as classrooms, assemblies or other places where there are quite a number of peers or people present. These scenarios are often at school and avoiding them can lead to students missing lessons and getting behind with work.

It can also become quite awkward when friends, peers or teachers begin to ask why you weren't in a particular lesson. You may have found that busy shopping centres, cinemas, restaurants and concerts may also be added to your 'no go' list over time. What these situations often have in common is that they are hard to get out of if you need to. Young people often talk about how hard it is to leave a classroom, as they are worried they won't be allowed or will be asked why they are going. Assemblies are also very hard to exit from, with lots of young people worrying they are drawing attention to themselves when they get up and leave.

As well as avoidance, we often try to control or avoid our panic symptoms in other ways, using panic traps, which we have talked about in previous chapters.

Example traps

- Take a bottle of water with you at all times.

- Take your mobile phone.

- Tell yourself to stop feeling a certain way.

- Avoid being alone in certain places.

- Only exercise with your Fitbit, which shows your heart rate.

- Constantly scan your body for symptoms.

- Always open a window in the car.

- Breathe in a certain way.

- Stay very still.

- Sit near the end of a row or near the door.

- Wear baggy clothing or a jacket to cover up.

- Make up excuses about why you can't go to certain places.

- Always take a certain route home.

- Push panic thoughts away.

All of these examples show ways that people use to control or stop panic symptoms from arising. Hopefully by now you have seen that the more we try to control these, the more likely it is that we bring them on and the worse we end up feeling.

Panic traps and avoidance keep panic symptoms going.

Remember the reptilian brain and the 'fight or flight' response? When we have panic feelings, if we think they are dangerous, our brain will tell us to get out – and quickly – or make us do things to feel more in control. If we feel we can't easily leave or that we don't have control, this leads to more anxiety and panic symptoms and so on. Ultimately it leads to you avoiding this situation next time around or doing lots of things to try to control the situation.

Why can't I simply avoid these situations?

You can, of course, just decide to avoid situations, but the problem is that you are probably missing out. Missing out on schoolwork, missing out on sport, socializing, shopping activities... We also know that young people who experience significant anxiety over a long period, and as a result miss out a lot on normal everyday activities, sometimes go on to develop low mood. This can be really debilitating and often then makes it harder to tackle panic symptoms. Remember our universal need for social contact we talked about in Chapter 2 – it is important we are able to find ways of having this.

Avoiding situations where you feel out of control can also take its toll. Yes, you can carry on being in full control and planning ahead for all eventualities. However, this takes a lot of energy, both mental and physical, and will probably also get in the way of friendships, relationships and getting other things done. Not to mention that it can be completely exhausting!

There is another reason though. We find that the avoidance leads to avoidance. First, you might miss Maths, then you notice some unpleasant feelings in Science and feel that you can't go to that lesson either. Another lesson might follow. Your 'fight or flight' response gets activated more and more, and your sense of freedom is completely lost.

Creating your freedom plan

So what can you do? You can start gradually to reduce your avoidance, drop your panic traps and face your fears – by doing the things that you have up to now avoided, or by relinquishing some control over these situations or by planning less. This is often referred to as 'graded exposure'. The idea being that you gradually, step by step, expose yourself to the fearful situations (and your panic symptoms) without doing anything to stop it. Like conducting experiments, this is also hard work! It means you will feel anxious and you will have panic sensations, but we will help you devise a graded plan so you can do this gradually rather than all at once.

Having said this, it is absolutely your call. You may decide that now is not the right time to start to work on this, and that is fine. Just be aware that this may in time have a negative impact. We hope that you have read about other ideas in this book that you have been able to use to help with some of your panic symptoms. If you decide at any time that you are ready to create your own freedom plan, just come back to this chapter and have a go!

What situations do you avoid?

The first step is to write a list of all the situations you currently avoid because of your panic symptoms (or situations you only put yourself in if you can use your panic traps).

Here are some examples:

Avoided situations

- Lessons
- Assembly
- Lecture hall
- Dentist
- Concert
- Football match
- Cinema
- Being a long way from home

- A long car journey
- Physical activities/exertion
- Being alone
- Small, enclosed spaces
- Restaurants
- Family gatherings
- Friends' houses

You can use the following table to write these situations, along with the anxiety rating you give them. Yours may be a very long list or quite a short one. It really doesn't matter; just try to include everything you can think of. In Chapter 3, you may have jotted down situations that trigger your panic sensations. These might also be situations that you avoid (or you use your panic traps in), so add these to your list here.

Situation avoided (or I can only face with my panic traps)	Anxiety rating
1.	
2.	
3.	
4.	
5.	
6.	
7.	
8.	
9.	

How anxious do you feel?

Rate your anxiety for each situation on your list. So, think about if you were in that situation now, how anxious you would feel on a scale of 0 to 10 (0 = completely fine, 10 = the most anxious you have felt), assuming that you do not use any of your panic traps. You may have to guess if you have not been in that particular situation for a while.

Which panic traps do you use?

The next step is to jot down all your panic traps. You may have done this in Chapter 3, so refer back, and write them down here too.

I only feel I can be in these situations as long as I:

1. ....

2. ....

3. ....

4. ....

5. ....

6. ....

We will come back to these shortly...

Now rank your avoided situations and begin to write out your freedom plan

Put the situations in order from least to most scary. Put the lowest rated ones at the bottom and work up to the higher rated ones, a bit like a ladder. Your graded plan is now beginning to take shape. What is the scariest situation? This is likely to be your ultimate goal. Is it the hardest challenge for you and one you would like to achieve? If so, it sounds like it would make a good ultimate goal. If not, think about what the biggest challenge might be (that you are happy to work towards) and put that at the top as your ultimate goal. For example, Georgia, a young person who experiences panic, would love to go to a concert of her favourite band.

Now think about which panic traps you use in each of these situations and note them down next to each step. Your aim is to try your best *not* to use them when you go into this situation.

Here is an example of Georgia's graded plan:

Step	Anxiety rating	Resisting panic traps
Ultimate goal: Concert	9	Don't take water, don't check exits, don't ask to sit on the end of the row
Step 7: Go to the cinema with friends	8	Don't take water, don't sit on the end, don't go to the toilet several times during the film
Step 6: Go to the cinema with my mum	7	Don't sit on the end, don't go to the toilet several times during the film
Step 5: Go shopping with friends	5	Don't take phone and spare charger
Step 4: Go for a run with a friend	4	Don't wear Fitbit, don't stop if getting a bit breathless
Step 3: Attend assembly	3	Don't sit on end, don't do special breathing
Step 2: Participate in hockey sessions	3	Try to run (not walk)
Step 1: Go to my Maths lesson	1	Don't ask the teacher in advance if I can leave to go to the toilet, don't take water

As you will see, Georgia's plan includes lots of different situations. Georgia's first step is one that she has done before (attending a Maths lesson) but does sometimes avoid it at the last minute if she starts to panic. She is going to try to attend every one if she can. It is a good idea for the first step to be something you have done quite recently, as this will give you confidence to try it again. When Georgia does one of these things, she is going to try *not* to engage in her panic traps, which she has listed next to each step. So, when she goes to Maths, she is going to try not to talk to the teacher at the beginning to ask him if she can leave if she needs to.

Now write out your freedom plan:

Step	Anxiety rating	Resisting panic traps
Ultimate goal:		
Step 7:		
Step 6:		
Step 5:		
Step 4:		
Step 3:		
Step 2:		
Step 1:		

Give it a go!

Start at the bottom and try each step a few times until your anxiety level has reduced and you feel okay. That does not mean you won't have any panic symptoms; you probably will. It may take longer than a few times for your anxiety to reduce enough for you to feel confident to try the next step, and that is absolutely fine. There is no rush, and moving slowly up your ladder is a good idea.

If you find you can only do the step if you do one of your panic traps, that is fine. That is still an achievement. Next time, try without your panic trap though!

Try to resist your panic traps when you complete each step.

Be on the lookout for your little critic. They may be telling you that you have to get up the ladder really quickly. Well, you don't; you can take as long as you need, and going slower tends to work better. What would you say to a friend who was struggling to move up their freedom plan? Say the same thing to yourself.

Just keep going until you reach your ultimate goal, although it doesn't matter if you don't get there. Managing any of the steps on your freedom plan is a great achievement.

What if I can't cope with my panic symptoms?

You will almost definitely have some panic sensations to start with. This is because there is probably now an association in your brain between a particular situation and certain physical experiences. Your brain is also likely to be on the lookout for any unusual or unpleasant sensations and immediately sees these as dangerous.

But remember what you learnt from doing your experiments: are these symptoms really dangerous or are they actually harmless? Can you cope well with them even if it feels like you aren't able to?

Draw on your new ability to accept and embrace. Say hi to your panic buddy – you don't need to do anything else.

Be sure to try to use some of the self-compassion skills as well. When your little critic appears, think about what you would say to a friend who might be struggling and say it to yourself. An attempt at a step on your plan, even if you have to exit early or don't complete it, is a great achievement.

Come up with a back-up plan

If you do need to leave a situation, or don't complete the step, that is okay. But sometimes, because you are worried that this is going to happen, you can't face trying the step in the first place. Having a back-up plan can help you give it a try.

Let's just imagine you are trying to do one of your steps (e.g. go to assembly) and the panic sensations become too much. Think about what you could do. What are your options? Of course you could do one of your panic traps, but we know these will ultimately keep your panic going, so try not to!

Back-up options may be talking to a friend who could try to calm you down, asking to go to the toilet, leaving the room without saying anything or phoning your mum for help. Think about what might work best for you in that situation, then plan what you would do. You might not need to use your plan, but it is there if you need it, and having the plan may reduce your anxiety enough to allow you to try the step in the first place.

A word of caution: if you are someone who really needs to control things, having a plan may be unhelpful. We are trying to encourage you to drop those panic traps that you use to take control (e.g. taking a water bottle with you). Having a plan could become a new form of control, so just be aware, and don't make one if you can do without it!

My back-up plan:

....

....

....

....

....

....

....

....

....

Reward yourself

Facing fears and experiencing panic symptoms is really hard work. We all need an incentive sometimes, particularly if we are doing something that is difficult. So think about how you can reward yourself for your efforts or get your parent/carer or a friend to do so. What could you treat yourself to if you manage to do a step, or if you tried it but didn't quite manage it? Could it be a bar of chocolate, a hot bath, watching a favourite movie? Keep an eye out for your little critic, who may tell you that you don't deserve a reward. Nonsense, you do. Please believe us!

Round up

Tackling situations that you have avoided, and not using your panic traps, is hard work but can really make a difference to lots of areas of your life. Devise a freedom plan, in a graded way, and try each step over and over before moving on to the next one. If you are really struggling to try a step, come up with a back-up plan in case it feels too overwhelming. The more you address your avoidance and drop your panic traps using your freedom plan, the easier it will get. Keep any eye out for your little critic and use your self-compassion skills. Remember to restore the balance, using the strategies in Chapter 6, after you have attempted a step.

Questions to get you thinking

1. *Do you want to stop avoiding certain things? If you did, what difference would it make to you?*

2. *Are there times you haven't used your panic traps? How did it work out?*

3. *Can you think of times you have managed to do really challenging things? What helped you?*

4. *Which strengths or characteristics do you have that you could use to help you face your fears?*

5. *How do you feel about rewarding yourself? Do you have reservations? If so, what are they and why do you have them?*

Chapter 9
Putting It All Together

We are now at the end of the book and hope you have discovered some new things about your panic and about yourself and been able to make some progress towards finding freedom from your panic. We have covered a lot of information and purposefully included a variety of ideas and approaches in order to give you the best possible chance of realizing you already have freedom from your panic within your reach.

If you have been using the 'questions to get you thinking' at the end of each chapter and have had the chance to apply some of the ideas, you may have already noticed a difference in your panic levels and your ability to cope when they arise. If so, that's great, and you are likely to experience even more breakthrough moments if you continue to use what you have learnt in your day-to-day life.

If you haven't yet given anything a go, now may be the right time to make sure you have fully understood what we are asking of you, to go back over the chapters and have another think about what you could apply at this point, or perhaps in the future. The great thing about having a book is that you can go over the material many times and revisit particular ideas at any point.

Claiming your freedom

At the start of this book, we made a bold statement and declared that freedom from panic is already yours. We absolutely believe this to be true and we hope that you have picked up the central message of this book: **the more you do to try to stop feeling panicky, the more trapped you become by panic.**

In fact, what we are really asking of you is to *do nothing* and *drop the effort and need to control*.

We know how difficult this idea can seem, and for many, especially those who have been fighting, battling and struggling with anxiety and their panic for a while, it can come across as far too simplistic. For those of you who may fall into this category, we would like you to take a moment to really consider the following:

- Has anything you have *done* to make your feelings and symptoms improve actually made a positive difference?

- Has *fighting and battling* your thoughts and feelings given you a sense of relief and security, or has it left you feeling exhausted and overwhelmed?

- Has *avoiding places or trying to figure out how to keep panic symptoms at bay* made your life more enjoyable, or has it kept you trapped and unable to do things you want or need to do?

From our countless conversations with those who struggle with panic and anxiety, we have a pretty good idea about what your answers to the above may be. You and many others have probably tried everything you can, up until this point, to respond and push back against panic. If you continue to carry that burden around with you, over time it will get heavier and heavier.

Our final invitation to you now is, therefore, to stop doing what you have previously done, make peace with the way your body responds to things and go about your day without changing a thing to please your panic buddy!

Finally, take a look again at how 'doing nothing' really is your best chance at claiming freedom from panic, and take some time to reflect on our final 'questions to get you thinking'.

Stop comparing yourself to others and trying to change things about yourself. BE YOU and ACCEPT and WELCOME your feelings and challenges (Chapter 4)

This is your journey and it's up to you what you are willing to try. There is NO PRESSURE to do anything different. Take time to process your new understanding (Chapter 8)

Enjoy a sense of calm and security as you relax your body and rest your mind (Chapter 6)

Be okay with not feeling okay (Chapter 5)

Be open to making new discoveries (Chapter 7)

Do nothing

Do what you like to do, despite feeling anxious (Chapter 8)

Remember that uncomfortable feelings and thoughts WILL PASS (Chapter 2)

Don't avoid situations or try to control things so that you don't feel panicky (Chapter 8)

Panic symptoms are part of our survival mechanisms. When they are activated, ACKNOWLEDGE THEM and they will pass on their own (Chapter 2)

Notice your anxious thoughts and the fears you have about your panic symptoms, but DON'T TRY TO STOP THEM. Just BE CURIOUS and see if they come true (Chapter 7)

Round up

We have covered a lot of different approaches in this book and we hope you will continue to have a go at trying out the techniques and ideas discussed. Take some time to go back over the chapters and read over any notes you may have made to help you. And most importantly, don't forget, freedom from panic is already yours.

Questions to get you thinking

1. How have you tried to control your panic, and what do you think have been your major panic traps?

2. What are the most important things you have discovered from reading this book and during your own reflections?

3. What things have you done that you thought would be helpful but have actually kept your panic going?

4. Are there positive aspects to your panic symptoms? What do you like about your panic buddy?

5. What new things have you discovered that you want to remember and develop further?

6. What are your intentions for the future?

GOOD LUCK AND ENJOY CLAIMING YOUR FREEDOM

Recommended Websites

Anxiety UK

www.anxietyuk.org.uk

A national organization run by those and for those with anxiety.

Be Mindful

www.bemindful.co.uk

Information about how mindfulness can reduce depression, anxiety and stress.

British Association for Behavioural and Cognitive Psychotherapies

www.babcp.com/public/what-is-cbt.aspx

Information about what cognitive behavioural therapy is.

www.cbtregisteruk.com

Register of practising cognitive and behavioural therapists in your area.

Mind

www.mind.org.uk

Provides advice and support to empower anyone experiencing a mental health problem.

NHS Guide to Yoga

www.nhs.uk/live-well/exercise/guide-to-yoga

The National Health Service's introductory guide to yoga.

Royal College of Psychiatrists

www.rcpsych.ac.uk/mental-health/parents-and-young-people

Information for young people, parents and carers about young people's mental health. Includes information about symptom criteria for a range of mental health problems.

The British Dietetic Association

www.bda.uk.com

The Association of UK Dieticians, which is the professional association for UK dieticians. Provides information for those seeking professional support and advice on healthy eating.

The British Psychological Society

www.bps.org.uk/public/find-psychologist

The British Psychological Society register of psychologists in your area.

The Compassionate Mind Foundation

www.compassionatemind.co.uk

The Compassionate Mind Foundation promotes wellbeing through compassion.

Yoga Alliance Professionals

www.yogaalliance.co.uk

Information and resources for those practising or wanting to learn more about yoga.

YoungMinds

www.youngminds.org.uk

The UK's leading charity fighting for children and young people's mental health.

Youth Mindfulness

www.youthmindfulness.org

Information about mindfulness courses for young people.